Land of My Ancestors

Land of My Ancestors

An epic South African story, based on true events

BOTLHALE TEMA

PENGUIN BOOKS

Published by Penguin Books
an imprint of Penguin Random House South Africa (Pty) Ltd
Reg. No. 1953/000441/07
The Estuaries No. 4, Oxbow Crescent, Century Avenue, Century City, 7441
PO Box 1144, Cape Town, 8000, South Africa
www.penguinrandomhouse.co.za

Penguin
Random House
South Africa

First published 2005
This edition published 2019

1 3 5 7 9 10 8 6 4 2

Publication © Penguin Random House 2019
Text © Botlhale Tema 2019

All rights reserved. No part of this publication may be reproduced, stored in a retrieval system or transmitted, in any form or by any means, electronic, mechanical, photocopying, recording or otherwise, without the prior written permission of the copyright owners.

Grateful acknowledgement is made to Sipho Sepamla, Mongane Serote, Njabulo Ndebele and Es'kia Mphahlele for permission to reproduce the poems on pages 1, 65, 129 and 189

PUBLISHER: Marlene Fryer
MANAGING EDITOR: Robert Plummer
EDITOR: Martha Evans
COVER DESIGNER: Ryan Africa

Set in 11 pt on 16.3 pt Simoncini Garamond

Printed by **novus print**, a Novus Holdings company

MIX
Paper from responsible sources
FSC® C022948

Penguin Random House is committed to a sustainable future for our business, our readers and our planet. This book is made from Forest Stewardship Council ® certified paper.

ISBN 978 1 77609 412 7 (print)
ISBN 978 1 77609 413 4 (ePub)

To

*Our great-grandfathers, Polomane and Maja,
who raked up the shards and gave rise to us*

*Our grandfather, Stephanus, who stepped out in the morning,
shook off the dew and blazed out a survival trail for us*

*Our father, Davidson, and uncle, Ernest,
who dared to paint life in their own colours*

With them ahead, we have no business to fail at life!

PROLOGUE

Land of My Ancestors was first published in 2005, with the title *The People of Welgeval*. It is a story about the land that my family used to inhabit, a remarkable place called Welgeval in the western Transvaal, now the North West province. It is a story of how my ancestors built a community there, how they came to own this land and how it was later taken away from them. In this new edition, I also describe how the land restitution process has been implemented in our area.

Apartheid South Africa was not known for encouraging free movement of black people. With the battery of pass and influx-control laws waiting to ensnare them, it was downright dangerous to venture too far from home. Yet my family ranks as one of the most nomadic black families in the country.

When I was a young girl, my father was a school principal in Phokeng near Rustenburg, and at the beginning of every weekend he would drive us to my maternal grandmother's house in nearby Tlhabane township, or to Welgeval, a farm in the Pilanesberg where he had grown up and where his parents still lived. Later, my father was promoted to school supervisor and was transferred to a series of rural towns in the western Transvaal. Our family became even more nomadic. The older children – including me – were put in boarding schools, and for a while my mother and my youngest sister lived at Welgeval, looking after my father's mother after her husband passed away. My father commuted between all these places where his family was scattered.

We adjusted to our lifestyle by forming loose attachments to places, with the result that even now I hate the question "Where do you come from originally?" because it demands a long explanation. But when forced to answer, I say that I come from all the small towns of the western Transvaal, but all my school holidays were spent in one place, Welgeval, the farm where my father was born. This was the only place that could claim my allegiance as my home. If places give people their identity, I got mine from Welgeval, an unusual place inhabited by a community in which nine out of ten people were my relatives.

The Friday-afternoon journeys from Phokeng to Welgeval are among my earliest memories. My father would undergo a transformation when he came home from work, took off his tie and prepared for his weekend farming duties: cattle dipping or calf branding, ploughing and planting during the rainy season. With a resolute step he would pack the van with groceries that my mother collected during the week, leaving space for the bags of cattle feed, salt, mielie meal and mielie seed – and his three children. I remember his concentration and focus when he got onto the main road from Phokeng, alert to the traffic police, who would dash onto the road as soon as they saw the rickety van coming along. A safe trip meant that Father didn't have to pull over and lay out a blanket to tinker under the vehicle, and that we weren't stopped by traffic cops who would strut around the van and ask the menacing question, "*Waarheen gaan dié hoenderhok?*" (Where is this fowl-run going?)

The van would lumber down the main road, past Boshoek, over the Kgetleng River bridge until we turned off the main road at Matooster about thirty miles from Phokeng. We then went on to farm roads, which required a different driving skill. I noticed my father's steering wheel constantly shifting and turning as he manoeuvred the bumps on the road, the bushes to the sides or the

Prologue

water gulley that ran alongside after the rains. With every twist and turn, Father's mood seemed to grow lighter. He would comment about how farmers didn't look after the roads; how he should bring the boys to come and help him pack stones on the road. Suddenly a hare or steenbok would hop in front of the car and Father would chase after it, careful not to drive over it but just to give it a tap so that we could pick it up for dinner. We usually arrived at Welgeval by sunset, happy with anticipation of seeing my grandparents, my cousins and all the other people we knew. Welgeval was a place of security and safety, because my people owned it and they set the rules, even though they also paid allegiance to the Bakgatla tribe.

Welgeval by day was a totally different place from night-time. The days were marked by distant looping sounds: a woman shouting across the valley to warn a "neighbour" about the cattle that she could see entering a field to destroy the crops; men in the fields, coaxing their cattle or donkeys to pull the ploughs or planters.

"*Thibelang dikgomo tseo!*"

"*Kom, Swartland! Kom, Kamaas!*" echoed between the hills.

In the background was a symphony of bird music: the calls of turtledoves and lourie birds, the squeaks of the starlings. Towards sunset the cowbells and bellows of cattle joined in and worked the music to a crescendo that died down as evening fell. Sunset announced the end of all activities of the day, and the nights, usually dark as pitch, walled families off from one another.

The old homesteads stood far apart and were barely visible from afar, even during the day. Interspersed between the homes were plough fields for each of the families. My grandparents' home faced a little farm school and church that stood at the bottom of the valley across the river.

Neighbours and relatives rarely saw one another during the week. The Sunday service at the little church not only catered to the spirit but provided entertainment as well. All able-bodied Welgevalers made sure they never missed a service. Each Sunday morning they would put on their Sunday best and trickle down the tributary footpaths from their homes to the church.

Different preachers took turns to conduct the service each week, except on *"nagmaal"* (communion) Sunday when the *dominee* from the main church in Moruleng came. One day during the service, my cousin Moloko suggested that we go around the pulpit to check if the preacher had his Bible the right way up. She had heard that some Welgeval preachers could not read but had memorised a few verses from the Bible and pretended to read them before preaching.

We thought we had a very funny story to tell our grandmother when we got home, but she was not amused at all. Instead she scoffed and scolded us. "You are laughing, *toe, lag maar*," she said. "You take so much for granted." We looked at each other and wondered what she meant by that.

Growing up on Welgeval, we all knew we were different. Firstly, there was no chief living in our community. Secondly, Welgeval men were dedicated and fierce cattle farmers who called each other *"neef"* (cousin) and the older people spoke a lot of Afrikaans. They grew crops such as sweet potatoes and mielies that were different from those grown in neighbouring villages. These crops, together with their cattle, were the means of barter trade with the neighbouring communities. The women looked after children, prepared food, kept homes clean – typical "women's work" – but they also kept pigs, which were slaughtered mainly in winter, and from the fat they collected they produced *"boereseep"* to wash their clothing. These were uncommon activities among black communities in the area. How it all got to be so different, nobody ever offered to explain. In fact, enquiring about these anomalies was an invitation to a smack. Whatever the story was, the old folks sat on it and made sure we never heard it from them.

Prologue

But the more tightly they kept the lid on our origins, the more curious we children became. As we grew older, we learnt indirectly that not only were we different, but we were also outsiders – we did not originate from within the mountains of Pilane where Welgeval was ensconced. Fragments of praise songs that old people recited at weddings hinted at a distant place in the northern Transvaal (today's Limpopo province) called "ga Moletji" – but no one explained the significance of this.

Welgeval was our home, with a support system for all circumstances and a regular life rhythm in all seasons. This regularity defined people's roles and lent a sense of belonging. Men ploughed and planted crops in spring; women weeded the fields in summer and did pottery when it was too hot to work in the fields; everybody harvested in winter and prepared produce to barter in neighbouring villages for crops we didn't produce ourselves. Education was of central importance: all children went to the local primary school before joining their parents in farming or going on to secondary school elsewhere. As farming on Welgeval grew more stable and successful, ambitious families encouraged their children to enter professions. My father set a non-negotiable rule that we should get a profession before we got married. Parents sometimes sold cattle to pay for their children's education.

But our habitation of Welgeval came to an end at the height of apartheid. In 1980 it was incorporated into the Pilanesberg National Park, and our people were moved away and resettled elsewhere. We lost a place that had nurtured our family for generations.

Many years later, I stumbled across intriguing information about Welgeval. I was secretary-general of the South African National Commission for UNESCO at the time, and one of my responsibilities was to facilitate the implementation of UNESCO projects in South Africa. I attended a meeting of the Slave Route project in

Cape Town, part of a global initiative to raise consciousness about the history of slavery and to set up economic development projects in the affected communities. At the time, I thought the only slaves in South Africa had been those whom the Dutch East India Company had brought to the Cape. The South African Slave Route project therefore focused mainly on slavery in the Cape.

At the meeting, I exhorted descendants of slaves in the Cape to embrace their history and not to be ashamed of it, arguing that feeling shame amounted to blaming the victims for their history. Later, after I told a historian friend about this, she handed me a book, *Slavery in South Africa*, to show me that slavery was not confined to the Cape. The book, edited by Elizabeth A. Eldredge and Fred Morton, outlines the history of slavery throughout South Africa, including in the Transvaal. It explains how the Boers used to raid villages in the northern Transvaal and bring back "black ivory" in the form of children and women to work on their farms. She pointed me to page 179, where Welgeval was mentioned:

When missionary Henry Gonin arrived in Rustenburg in 1862 for the purpose of establishing a DRC station in the area, he encountered ex-slaves in Rustenburg town and on the surrounding farms. At Welgeval, where Gonin opened his first station, his first enquirers were Dutch-speaking Africans who had grown up in Boer farms and homes. Among them were "Januari", who worked for Gonin as a servant and interpreter and was eventually christened "Petrus", and Vieland, christened "Stephanus" by Gonin. When a boy, January was among the women and children stolen by a large Boer commando during the raid on the BaKwena capital of Dithubaruba, near Molepolole in 1852. Vieland too was captured when young.[1]

Prologue

I couldn't believe it. "Welgeval, that's my home!" I said. "I spent many good years of my youth there and you are telling me I'm a descendant of a slave!"

I couldn't put down the book that night as I uncovered the most unexpected information about my people. In one of his chapters, Fred Morton says that the history of slavery in the Transvaal was never openly acknowledged, even by most historians, partly because legal slavery was abolished in 1834 by the British who governed the Cape then, and because the Boer leaders in the Transvaal signed the Sand River Convention of 1852, which agreed to prohibit slavery. This meant that officially no slavery was permitted in the Cape after 1834 or in the Transvaal after 1852. However, Morton says that the reality was quite different:

> *as late as the 1870s on the fringes of the Transvaal, slave raids on the Setswana-, Sesotho-, and Nguni-speaking peoples were conducted. Along the moving horizon of the "Great Trek", peoples living in the eastern and northern Cape, Orange Free State, and Natal were attacked and seized. Most of the slave raiders were Boers aided by their African allies, and most of the Africans they captured were children. Young captive laborers, often bound to Boer households and raised to adulthood without parents or kin, helped to sustain and consolidate the advancing Dutch frontier.*

Another contributor to the book, Jan C.A. Boeyens, writes that this "new" form of slavery was euphemistically called "apprenticeship" or *"inboekstelsel"*. The captured children were referred to as *"inboekelinge"*, because their presence in the Transvaal had to be recorded, or as *"weeskinders"* (orphans), a false explanation of why they were separated from their parents. They were also called *"kleingoed"* (little ones), *"buit"* (booty) and "black ivory", as opposed to the real white ivory that the Boers collected from the northern Transvaal where they also raided for cattle.[2]

Morton writes that an important characteristic of the *inboekelinge* was their assimilation of the Dutch culture: they spoke mainly Dutch or Afrikaans, and they were adept at most Dutch household chores (cooking, butter- and soap-making) and economic activities (tannery, carpentry, gun and wagon repair). These were some of the activities practised by my people at Welgeval.

Officially, the *inboekelinge* were not supposed to be ill-treated, but reality differed from policy. According to Morton, "*the evidence indicates that ZAR [Zuid Afrikaanse Republik] officials ignored the code, just as they had violated legal prohibitions against slave raiding and slave trading and recognized the absolute authority of an individual Boer owner over the inboekelinge as property.*"[3]

Jan Boeyens reports the following account by Reverend Charles Murray, the Dutch Reformed Church mission inspector, during a visit with missionary Henry Gonin to the northern Transvaal. They encountered a man who was on his way to sell children to other Boers in the Transvaal. Murray wrote:

> *Gert Duven(h)age, son of T, previously of Hope Town ... had a strange cargo that he was going to trade. In the back of the wagon I saw about eight small African children packed tightly together, in the same manner, that I as a child, was wont to observe in drawings of slave ships ... It appeared that he had traded them "at the back" for two head of cattle each, and that they would be traded "ahead" for six head of cattle each. In the meantime they were being badly treated, one can even say abused. At night in the bitter winter cold they lay on the bare ground in the open sky, some even with their bodies naked. The youngest child was, I would say, not more than four years old,*

Prologue

and many times it was heart-rending to hear them cry during the night because of the cold.[4]

As I read Eldredge and Morton's book, I could see how the people of Welgeval fitted the description of *inboekelinge*. I could appreciate the history of cruelty in South Africa because we experienced it in different forms under apartheid. What I could not wrap my head around was how I had grown up happy: how did my people transform that amount of pain and trauma from their past to produce me, who felt privileged by my upbringing? My assumptions of who I was lay shattered. There was no privilege, but an immense debt to those who really suffered. The true meaning of Welgeval to my people began to emerge – it must have been a place of refuge for people who had escaped slavery and oppression.

From then on, I became obsessed with the need to document our story for generations to come because Welgeval is no longer there for them to experience it. I interviewed the older relatives and pieced together the fragments of information we could gather and produced a narrative of the people of Welgeval.

As I scoured the archives and libraries to establish the ownership of Welgeval, I came across issues relating to land ownership for black people following the 1913 Land Act. The story of Welgeval is thus also a story of land ownership – how the people of Welgeval bought the farm, how they nearly lost it and how they finally lost it. Thankfully, the story does not end with a complete loss. In the epilogue to this book, I will tell the story of the land claim concerning Welgeval and the complexities that arose because Welgeval lies inside a conservation park.

When I first wrote this book, I decided to write it in the form of a historical novel. I wanted to tell the story in such a way that our children would read it and get the taste and feel of the place.

Botlhale Tema

I wanted them to understand the story of our survival and reinvention. I decided to bring the main characters of Welgeval to life and animate the history from my experience and the information I gleaned from my interviews and research. I inserted the kind of dialogue I used to hear on Welgeval. The story of the capture of the main characters and their lives before settling on Welgeval is a surmise of what could have happened to them based on the research of events surrounding slavery in the Transvaal. However, the description of events following settlement on Welgeval is true in that it is based on archive material, interviews I conducted and my own experience. All the main characters were real – Polomane David Moloto was my great-grandfather and his son Stephanus was my grandfather. Davidson Polomane Moloto was my father.

PART I

O! spirits of my ancestors awake
I hear the whizz of bullet words
and am felled as many times as I listen
give me the silence of your graves

SIPHO SEPAMLA
TO MAKANNA AND NONGQAWUSE

1

For days on end a dry southeaster raged, riding roughshod over wisps of clouds that dared to gather in the sky. Parched of all crop and green, the fields lay abandoned at the bottom of the valley. The wind lifted the loose red soil from the empty fields and suspended it like a curtain against the rocky hills on which the village of Moletji nestled, cutting off all view of the horizon. Too weak to move, the cattle spent their hours lying under the few thorn trees that withstood the inhospitable weather. Occasionally, they staggered up to pick at the sour needle leaves like goats. Ploughs and hoes lay idly under piles of tired soil in Moletji's backyards.

It had not rained for two seasons in a row. Small stock died daily, and at first the people secretly celebrated the unexpected supply of meat, which was normally a delicacy reserved for special occasions. But soon they found themselves unable to deal with all of it. The women tried to dry some, but it was simply foolish to leave it hanging outside in the hot and gritty wind. Rotting carcasses began to accumulate and an acrid stench lingered in the air, defying the invading southeaster. A blanket of doom hovered over Moletji with no sign of subsiding.

Chief Moloto was concerned. This was no ordinary drought, he thought. There was too much malice in the howling wind, which left no life in its wake. It could speak only of one thing: serious ancestral wrath. Feeling inadequate about approaching his ancestors on his own, he summoned his advisors to a meeting at his *kgotla* one morning. Ten representatives attended (one for each clan), taking their rightful seats in the *kgotla* circle, with the most senior, Mabona and Letsoalo, on either side of the chief. By special instruction, no one brought their usual pieces of leather to work on during the meeting. The chief wanted their full attention.

With a quick cursory greeting, he went straight to the point.

"Men, I've called you to come and help me look at the disaster that has gripped our village," he announced. "In all my life, I have never experienced drought as ferocious as this. The forefathers are not pleased."

The men stirred uneasily at the suggestion, which they knew the chief would not make lightly. It was only in times of serious trouble that such conclusions were drawn.

"What is the misdemeanor behind it?" the chief asked, raising his voice to gain the *kgotla*'s attention. "Will we ever be able to heal this rift between ourselves and our departed?"

Chief Moloto stopped suddenly and hung his head for a while, his sizeable belly heaving now and again. His men, fearing an angry response to any untimely intervention, were still. Finally, he raised his head and adjusted his leopard-skin cloak as he called for comments.

The gathering bubbled into life as the men muttered among themselves, offering various reasons for the drought. Sefara, an ambitious man who was ever eager for the chief's approval, leapt up to speak.

"The ancestors never turn their backs on us for no reason," he said shrilly. "Our hands are soiled; we must cleanse them!"

"That, Sefara, is clear enough for all to see," the chief sighed. "Anyone with half the brain of a dying dog can tell you that. The question is: What have we done to bring this upon ourselves?"

Again the men turned to one another, muttering over the matter, until Mabona, a rather wordy counsellor, stepped in to make his point.

"Chief, your words have hit the truth," he began. "It pains me that your trusted doctor Mapadimole has been so unsuccessful in getting reprieve from your ancestors ... I feel our situation is dire enough to require unusual measures. We are caught between the horns of an ox. We have, on this hand, our tribal pride ..." Mabona gestured with his right hand, and in unison the gathering tilted their heads, following his action, "... and then on this hand ..." The communal gaze turned to the left. "... there is our survival. But if we look at it plainly, our choice, Chief and dear compatriots, is simple ..."

"Mabona!" the chief barked with irritation. "Stop going round in circles like a sick cow! Come to the point."

"Lion of the north, my point is this," he responded. "I think we should drop our pride and enlist the help of the one whose skills are known far and wide, Queen Modjadji of the Balobedu, the ultimate rainmaker."

Suddenly he paused to check the response and quickly added, "I humbly submit that you consider calling her to come to our aid."

Slowly, without moving his head, the chief turned his gaze to the left where Mabona was sitting, his squint right pupil almost disappearing under his nose. He flicked his whisk and thrashed an invisible fly rather violently.

"Mabona, I can see that you don't know me well," he growled, narrowing his eyes to the size of a cobra's. "What gives you the idea that I can hand over the responsibility bestowed on me by my forebears to some, some, some ...?"

He flicked his whisk again, this time in Mabona's direction, as if to fling him out of his sight.

"In this village," he continued, "I alone can intercede for my people. The day some stranger takes over this duty, my body will be lying cold and dead on the floor. I hope I shall never hear this foolish if not downright wicked suggestion ever again. You are lucky, Mabona, that all your animals are dead or I would have fined you to the last one."

Mabona's cousin, Letsoalo, quickly jumped in to cool the brewing quarrel.

"Chief, let us not get sidetracked," he said, steering the chief's gaze away from Mabona. "In my opinion, our indiscretion is not hard to find. It's been three years since we last sent boys out to the mountain school. Not since the rumour began. We must expect to pay for violating our tradition. The forefathers will not smile at this."

As soon as Letsoalo made mention of the issue, two other men stood up to confirm the effect of this rumour, causing a loud murmur to erupt in the *kgotla*.

A rumour about strangers abducting children was running wild in the villages, with the result that parents simply refused to let their children out of their sight, disrupting the lifestyle and education traditions of the village. Word came first from the village of Matlala that young women collecting water from the river and herd boys had simply and inexplicably disappeared. Similar whispers came from surrounding villages.

"*Tsie lala.* Quiet," the chief commanded. "Letsoalo, yours are sensitive words. Even though I understand what you are saying, we must be careful not to antagonise our people. We cannot ignore their fears."

The men stared back at the chief in stony silence, clearly worried about the difficult situation they were facing. Satisfied that he had at least consulted his advisers for a solution, the chief closed the meeting with the conclusion that it was now time to approach the ancestors with his trusted guide and doctor Mapadimole. Mapadimole was responsible for opening communication with the departed spirits of the village, and shared with the chief the responsibility for rainmaking.

Just before sunset, the chief sent out an emissary to request a consultation. The doctor had been expecting the chief's call since hearing of the extraordinary meeting earlier in the day, and he had his special costume prepared for the occasion.

As the sun set, he slowly adorned himself in suitable ritual attire. He placed his lion-skin hat upon his head, and swathed his arms in armbands made up of a selection of feathers from the birds of the marshes. Next, he circled his wrists in a variety of bracelets that had been fortified in secret potions. These would strengthen his hands for successful handling of the cowrie shell. Finally, he slipped his feet into the leather sandals made from skin drawn from the forehead of one of the chief's dead oxen.

Before stepping out of his hut, Mapadimole took a bite of a bitter root to focus his mind and cupped his face in his hands for a minute, dispatching his spirit to alert the ancestors of the meeting. Then he grabbed his divination bag and made his way to the chief's homestead.

Mapadimole entered the chief's compound through the back entrance and headed straight to the secret hut, which was especially reserved for these types of meetings. The chief was waiting for him patiently in front of a small fire burning in the middle of the hut. This was a special fire made from dry branches of willow trees that grew on the banks of a local stream. Mapadimole settled himself down opposite the chief and greeted him.

"Chief, your servant has heeded your call."

"Man of Bakwena," the chief started, without lifting his eyes from the fire, "I don't have to explain the reason for my call. Our forefathers have turned their backs on us. Throw light on it so that we can make amends."

Mapadimole squatted and laid out his divination mat. He then shook his cowrie shell in the pouch and swiftly blew into it. He threw it down to have a first read. The doctor raised his eyebrows. He was not impressed.

"That's just the first pulse," he consoled himself, quickly collecting the bones and cupping them in his hands. Slowly, he blew into his palms, at the same time pleading with the chief's ancestors for a clearer vision. To get their support, Mapadimole asked the chief to blow on the bones as well, while he called out the chief's ancestors' names, one after another, as far back as he could remember. Once he'd completed the lineage, he threw down the bones for the first true reading.

Mapadimole groaned.

"Chief of Bakwena, son of Ramonamane," he sighed. "I don't like what I see."

He adjusted his seat to make himself more comfortable and leant forward to examine them more closely. Still he wasn't happy with their configuration. And so he decided to adjust his vision. Mapadimole dipped his fingers into his bag and collected a pinch of herbs, which he threw into the fire. A greenish flame leapt up and a thick black smoke billowed, stinging their eyes.

Mapadimole's eyes widened, stretching their socket muscles. He shook his head.

"My master, if you will allow me, I'd like to have time alone with them!" he cried.

Without a word, Chief Moloto stood up and went to bed.

2

A woman's scream pierced the still of the night. As flames shot up from blazing huts, mothers carried babies and dragged older siblings outside, shouting into the dark. In the light of the waning moon, shadowed riders could be seen torching the village, their faces hidden by hats and their features distorted by the blaze. Chief Moloto grabbed his spear and hurried his youngest son out of their burning hut. One of the horsemen met him at the door and smashed his head with the back of his rifle. As the chief slumped to the ground, his eldest son, who had been evacuating the villagers, stepped up and hit the offending horseman with a *kierie*. But his blow was too weak. The horseman about-turned and shot him straight through the heart, and then bent down to pick up the boy. He hauled him up onto the pommel of the saddle and held him with one arm while he continued shooting with the other. Two villagers saw this and jumped into the courtyard to rescue the chief's son, but the rider directed his horse out of the homestead and rode into the darkness. Angry and frustrated, the villagers then attacked any of the enemy they could find. They speared them repeatedly until they were blood-soaked. But for every horseman that fell, four villagers were shot.

Pools of blood gathered in between the scattered bodies, and in this howling pandemonium, some of the horsemen rounded up more children. Twelve men rode off with two children each. Older children (of about fourteen years of age) were placed in front of the rider, where they held sacks into which younger ones had been bundled. A few horsemen remained behind, shooting wildly to distract attention from the abductors, making sure that their colleagues were not followed. The villagers of Moletji, realising the invincible ferocity of the enemy and the terrible truth of the rumour, fled to the hills.

The horsemen waited until the village was deserted and then rode north to join the party with the children. Every so often, one of the men would dart out eastwards or westwards to check the lie of the land and to see if anyone was following.

With the pommel of the saddle jutting into his buttocks, Chief Moloto's son glimpsed a final sight of his father's village. In the distance, he thought he heard a woman shout his name into the night.

"Maja!" the voice called, "Maja!"

But the sound receded with the burning flames.

※

On the morning after the raid on Moletji, Jan Cloete took to the west to reconnoitre. He rode up to a little rocky outcrop that stood out like a wart on an otherwise flat land. At the top he dismounted on a smooth rock that jutted out to form a perfect platform for his purpose. He could see smoke rising from the morning fires in the village of Molepo, not so far away. Satisfied that there was no sign of any belligerence, he opened his fly buttons to relieve himself. Only two of the original four buttons left, he noted.

Jan was part of a band of fortune-seekers who in August 1852 had joined Paul Kruger's commando to support Potgieter in a raid against Chief Sekwati of the village of Phiring. Such raids were common, and Kruger's commandos frequently confiscated cattle by way of punishment.

On their return from the raid, Jan and a small group of men broke away from the rest of the commando, which was slowly driving Kruger's booty of confiscated cattle southwards. They took the chance to collect their own loot and decided to hit the nearest village, which happened to be Moletji; only this time they were anxious to seize "black ivory" and not cattle. Slaves from the north were popular with the farmers in the centre of the Transvaal Republic and further south in the Orange Free State up to the Cape. They always fetched a good price, because the farmers were satisfied that they would not run away like the locals. Generally, women and children were considered the best type of black ivory.

In the midst of his release, Jan heard a cough from under the rock on which he was standing. Startled, and barely managing to fasten one of his fly buttons, he reached for his rifle and barked an order for the fugitives to come out. Flashing images of his friends with spears sticking out of their torsos strengthened his resolve to shoot to kill.

A young boy and his mother had been collecting firewood in the veld when they heard the sound of an approaching horse. No one in the village of Molopo owned a horse and, with so many rumours about strange horsemen and their exploits in the villages, they were scared. As the horse approached, the pair scrambled under the rock ledge to hide until the danger had passed. But the horse stopped right above their hiding place. They crawled deeper into the little cave and huddled together quietly. The boy, Lesiba, started feeling an irritation in his throat from the dust he had inhaled while breaking the dry branches. He tried to suppress the impending cough, but it just got worse. Then he decided to cough a little with his mouth closed, just to clear the irritation. It was the wrong decision, for almost immediately a voice boomed from above, "*Kom uit, ek sê, kom uit!*"

The boy and his mother did not understand what the man was saying, but they could sense the command as they saw the nose of the rifle push back the bushes at the mouth of the cave. Lesiba's mother emerged first, hoping to beg for mercy, but before she could utter a word Jan Cloete let rip a shot and swiftly reloaded in anticipation of another troublemaker. Lesiba lurched towards his mother, screaming as she fell to the ground. Realising that this was only a child, Jan decided not to shoot, but he could not risk letting him go. Moreover, he could join the other children and increase Jan's earnings. He grabbed the child under his armpit, slung him over the front of his horse and trotted back to join the other riders.

3

"*Foei*, what a stink!" Jan Cloete shouted in disgust. "Get out and go and clean yourselves. Wash my sacks while you are at it," he added as he let the younger children out of the bags.

To his horror, Maja saw his younger sister Motumi emerge from one of the sacks. Jan waved them off in the direction of the river, and they ran and jumped in to wash off their collective embarrassment.

After relentless riding, the party had reached the Crocodile River, where they had selected a secluded spot on its banks to have breakfast and wait for the rest of Paul Kruger's commando. The men had fastened their horses to the surrounding trees and released the children to rest and bathe.

While the children were bathing, some of the men went to collect kindling to make fire for coffee, but Jan elected to take a nap instead. Maja, noticing that the men's attention was diverted, decided to sneak into the bushes and go back home to get help. Driven by concern for his sister, he was determined to find his older brother and round up the men of the village so that they could spring a surprise attack on the commando.

Jan's men returned to start the fire, and Piet Vermaak was just getting it going when he observed something strange about the children.

"Jan," he asked, "what are those children staring at?"

"What?" Jan replied curtly, annoyed by the disturbance.

"Something's moving under those trees. Over there, at the far end," Vermaak continued. "I think they startled a buck when they got in."

"Good for us, good breakfast! Hand me my gun. I'll go and fetch it," Jan said, gesturing towards his rifle. He stood up and walked towards the children, heading straight in the direction of the movement.

Just as he was about to shoot, the children screamed, and, surprised by their reaction, Jan went into the bush to check. He returned, dragging Maja along, and called all the other children out of the river. Ordering them to sit in a circle and watch, he lay Maja down in the middle. Then he fetched his riding crop and flogged the boy until his shoulder ached. With the first few strokes, Maja screamed, but then he realised it wasn't going to help; it would just annoy the man more. So he decided to focus his attention on Jan's toes, sticking out of his tattered boots. He watched them claw the sole as each blow was delivered. The harder the blow, the deeper they dug into the boot.

But Maja had misread the man. Jan resented the boy's silence and doubled his effort, until at last Maja started to yell again. He lifted his head to beg Jan to stop, but his language was unsuited to convey pain to this stranger. Their eyes locked, and Jan stopped for a moment to check the effect on the other children's faces. They stared back, their eyes swimming in tears. This only spurred him on, for he took off again and continued the beating until blood flowed down Maja's narrow back. Slowly, the screaming turned to groaning and finally uncontrollable retching.

Jan delivered the last couple of strokes to emphasise his point and then stopped, satisfied that none of the other children would want to experience what they had just witnessed. He shooed them back to the river so he could drink his coffee in peace.

The rest of the commando joined them just after breakfast. They arrived on horseback, some driving ox-wagons loaded with guns and real ivory. After coffee they decided on another day's rest before they set off on the slow journey to Rustenburg.

At first cock's crow the next morning, the men cleared one of the ox-wagons and loaded the children, this time tying them together – one arm of the younger children tied to one of the older ones.

4

On and on the rumbling wagons trundled the wide expanse of veld, flattening young elephant grass and grinding pebbles to sand. The men were determined to eat up the daily *skof* of eight miles in order to reach Rustenburg in three days. Towards sunset they found a water source and set up camp for the night. A mangled thicket of karee trees near the spring offered just the right kind of shelter.

Jan Cloete ordered the men to outspan the wagons and untie the children. He decided to stretch his legs and fetch firewood while the men were busy. When he had rolled in enough logs to keep the fires steady for the night, he found a secluded spot to sit down and unwind – away from the others.

The evening was cool and golden, bathed in the glow of the sun as it slipped behind the horizon. After so many trips to the north, Jan could foretell, from any location on the long journey, the exact spot where the sun would finally retire, and so he found a good position from which to watch it disappear. In summer the sun moved directly west, lingering longer over western towns and creating a lazy twilight in which farmers and their wives enjoyed cups of coffee after a hard day. There it was now, looping down the Rustenburg sky, spraying a blaze of pinks, purples and crimson in its wake.

At home, on these long summer evenings, Jan always felt broody. But it was easy to avoid melancholy on expeditions, because at this time he and his band would usually be mellow, if not completely drunk, from several gallons of *brandewyn*. But today they were unhappily sober, having polished off their supplies when they'd fortified themselves for the job at Moletji. So Jan succumbed to his usual morbidity. He took off his boot to remove a thorn picked up during the skirmishes at Sekwati's village. Half the soles were completely worn out. It was only thanks to the laced-up sturdy uppers that he could still keep them on his feet.

Jan had lived on and off with different Boer families around Rustenburg since their arrival from the Cape. It was now three years since he'd settled down as a tenant *bywoner* on district veldkornet Herklaas Malan's farm, and periodically he joined Kruger's commando when it set off to the north to sort out cheeky native chiefs. These trips were a source of hope for Jan's deeply longed-for future.

The man had never had family. There wasn't a relative to speak of. By the time he was conscious of these things, he was already living with whoever would have him. He didn't know what had happened to his parents or if he had any siblings. And so he watched family life in Malan's house with a lot of envy. Sometimes after work, when they parted from the fields, Jan would follow Malan home, pretending that he had farm matters to discuss with him, but secretly hoping that the family atmosphere would wash away his loneliness. Now, with the loot that he had brought from the north, he felt that he was getting closer and closer to his dream of a farm and family of his own.

While Jan was nursing his emptiness, Piet Vermaak loosened the knots that bound the children together. Inertly, three of them slithered to the ground.

"*Opskud!*" Piet shouted, as he gave each one a kick on their feet.

But the children remained prostrate.

Jan's reverie was disrupted by the commotion and he jumped up to check what it was about. Three bodies were lying on the ground.

"*My vaderland*, what's going on here?" he asked.

Jan reached down to shake the children, but their eyes continued to stare blankly at the sky, their heads lolled back. As he was struggling with them, the other children came and gathered round him and their immobile peers. Twenty-two pairs of enquiring eyes bore through Jan's back for an answer, but he had none to offer.

Jan and his men picked up the three limp bodies and pushed through the bystanders to go and lay them down under a tree on the further end.

Maja and two of the boys to whom the dead children had been tied started whimpering and rubbing their wrists. This vexed Jan. "Enough of this!" he shouted. "Go to bed."

The children slunk off in silence and huddled together under their assigned tree to sleep. Muted sobs were soon followed by gentle escapist snores, which signalled to the men to dispose of the bodies in the veld. Without tools to dig a grave, they put them together and piled branches on top of them in a semblance of decency before the wild animals could help themselves to the meat.

5

The rest of the journey was a little easier on the children. Jan and his men decided to keep them untied. He puzzled over the deaths all the way to Rustenburg. Never in five years of expeditions to the north had something like this happened. The children often tried to run away, an event for which the men were always prepared. But losing three like that was more than just a setback.

On arrival in Rustenburg, they headed for the veldkornet's farm to get the "orphans" booked before distribution to farmers. Children brought from the north in this manner were officially called orphans. "How did they get orphaned?" the missionaries from the London Missionary Society questioned critically. They insisted that the illegal importation of children was nothing but slavery on the sly, much to the annoyance of the Boers.

To regulate the distribution of such orphans and to appease the missionaries, the Boer authorities signed the Sand River Convention, stipulating that:

> *Whoever obtains a child or orphan, of whosoever he may have obtained it, he must register it. The landdrost or Veldkornet must make enquiry in what manner any one has become possessor of such a child. If everything is in order, the child must be registered, and then remain as a servant, till it shall have reached the age of 25, and shall then, as of age, become entirely free from all forced obligation to any service.*

The veldkornet's clerk placed a table under the tree in the yard, and Jan and his men lined the children up in front of it. The five girls stood at the back of the queue behind the boys. Jan Cloete stationed himself next to Maja to direct him on what to do after his name was called.

"August!" the clerk called as he wrote the name of the current month after which the first boy was named. The young Lesiba was pushed to the right.

"September!" the clerk called next. Vermaak jostled a young boy of about ten two steps to the right of the queue.

It later took only a tap on the shoulder for the rest of the boys to step aside after their names were called.

Thus with a shove and the stroke of a pen the children lost their names and gained new ones. The boys were named after the months of the year, starting with the one of their arrival. The clerk then repeated the cycle so that there would often be two or more Septembers. But this did not create a problem, as the boys usually went to different farmers, and if they happened to land up with the same one, the farmers distinguished one from the other by means of their physical features. One would, for instance, be called *Kort* or *Lang* September. The girls were bestowed with names from the Bible or any Dutch names the clerk could remember: Anna, Maria, Martha, etc.

Maja got the name April, and his younger sister was called Christina.

After booking, the children were on record as the *inboekselings* or *inboekelinge* (those who have been booked). The men who had "rescued" the "orphans" could then distribute them to interested parties, and it was at this point that the raids of African villages paid off, justifying Jan's hope for a better future.

The farmers gathered for the auction to begin. Black ivory was exchanged for farming implements, livestock and sometimes money for the traders' own farms. Jan began with the girls, knowing they would fetch a better price, as they were so few. He called the first girl forward and the farmers made their offers. When the bidding was over, the girl went off with the farmer whose offer had won. April watched his sister disappear with a farmer who won her because of the calf he had offered. Christina screamed and tried to pull away, but the farmer dragged her off, and the auction continued.

The whole process took about two hours. But a slight tussle ensued over the last remaining girl – a well-built and obedient-looking twelve-year-old whom two farmers had been eyeing from the beginning of the proceedings.

Otherwise, the event ran smoothly, and with very little ceremony the children dissolved into their new lives. For a plough and a cast-iron pot, a farmer by the name of Andreas Erasmus bought April and a young girl called Maria.

6

Erasmus and the two children arrived at the farm just as the sun was setting. Maria and April were to join a young slave girl, Sara, and a little boy, Augus, whom Erasmus had bought in circumstances he preferred to forget. With the new additions, he would have four pairs of young hands to groom for work on the farm. Already Augus was adept with the care of the goats, almost making up for the embarrassment Erasmus had suffered when his wife insisted he bid for a pregnant woman. How his friends had laughed at him, especially since it was in the middle of the reaping season. But his wife was adamant that it was a good investment: for the price of one they would end up with two servants.

Erasmus couldn't live down the embarrassment when the woman died soon after the boy was born, but fortunately the Boer expedition to Molepolole in Bechuanaland brought back a few young women, and the couple quickly made up for their loss. They got one called Tsholofelo, and immediately changed the name to Sara, a decision they also lived to regret, because a few months after the acquisition, Erasmus's sister, also called Sara, came up from the Cape to visit. She was not pleased to share a name with a slave, and for two months they had to resort to whistling to call the slave girl until the "real" Sara left.

Sara could hardly contain her joy over the new arrivals. Hastily, she fetched them and led them straight to the outer house where she stayed. She was especially pleased to have a young girl for company, because the Erasmus farm was buried deep in the middle of the Pilanesberg mountains, and only men ever went out on errands.

The following morning Sara took the children to meet Mevrou Erasmus. Along with small stock, Tina Erasmus was in charge of the women and child labour on the farm. Sara and the children found her sitting at her usual spot next to the wall on the eastern side of the house. Like a lizard, Tina seemed to need the warmth of the sun to get herself going at the beginning of the day.

"This wretched hip!" she would complain as she limped out of the house each morning and deposited her bulk on the *riempiestoel* next to the wall. She bent forward and rested her arms on her thighs to expose her back to the sun. Slowly, as it grew warmer and her muscles relaxed, Tina would straighten up, finally resting her back against the wall to sun her chest.

She was halfway through this process when the children arrived.

"*Môre*, Missus," Sara greeted.

"Humph ..." Tina grunted, and continued staring inertly at the ground.

"I've brought the children, Mevrou," Sara went on.

Tina's eyes grazed the ground and alighted at the children's feet. She shuffled her rear to adjust herself to the *riempies*, which were now digging deep into her fleshy buttocks. Finally, she took in a deep breath and said hoarsely, "Take them inside. I'll see them later."

Tina gulped another breath of air and heaved her chest up one more time for her back to reach the wall. This initial greeting set the tone for life on the Erasmus farm.

It was uncertain when Tina's discomfort was greater – mornings or evenings. The mornings seemed better, because her mood thawed with the gradually warming day. But it froze right down again towards evening as it got cooler. Young Augus gave her reports about the goats at sunset after shutting them in the kraal. Tina's ears were always piqued for any mistake, and at the slightest hint of one, she shouted, "*Op die vloer!*" and young Augus would throw himself at her feet. Tina would then flay his backside with the *platriem* created especially for whipping children.

Sometimes her husband's smelly boots would set her off, and Tina would lay into Andreas. But more often it was Sara's food. Tina believed that Sara was trying to poison her with the food she cooked, even though she had taught her how to prepare *boerekos*. It was impossible to please Tina at any time, worse still in the evenings. She was always sure to find something to lash out against to deflect her thoughts from her pain. Arthritis and a hip injury she had sustained during the trek from the Cape made a volatile mix for her emotional well-being.

When they left the Cape, Tina was as tall and strong as any of the men. She stood her ground and might have done even better had she not had the constant bother with her clothing. Always having to take care not to trip on her long skirt while she was busy with the men split her concentration. It almost cost her her life when they were pulling one of the wagons out of a ditch during their trek over the Matroosberge. She stepped on her hem and slipped, following the wagon into the ditch and landing on her hip, which was less padded at the time. Her hipbone cracked, and none of the known Boer remedies was ever able to relieve her from the ensuing pain. From that day on, Tina Erasmus became the tetchiest woman north of the Vaal River. This, at least, was what her husband thought. But he now believed that Tina's moods had taken on a life of their own, completely divorced from the original pain.

As time went by, Erasmus grew less and less willing to put up with his wife's moods. He started spending as much time away from home as he could afford. He was always seen leaving either on a hunt with his neighbours or to help the veldkornet with district duties.

One day, Andreas Erasmus set off quietly before Tina woke up, as he usually did. Unfortunately, this was to be his last trip. A cobra bit his horse, and Erasmus was thrown off. The horse then stomped on him repeatedly as it reacted to the snake poison. His friends brought back his corpse for burial on the farm.

April took the news of Erasmus's death rather badly. Erasmus had been something of a buffer between Tina and the children – or at least he had at times diverted attention away from them. But the boy needn't have worried, for subsequent events brought about a change of fortune.

Ben Oelofse had just finished his last seasonal job on different farms in the Boshoek district when he heard of Erasmus's accident. He was thus free to go and help with the funeral and perhaps lend a shoulder for the grieving widow to cry on. He stayed on after the funeral and helped with the dipping of the cattle. Tina Erasmus noticed and, being a practical woman, decided, "What the hell, if it's not him, it'll be some other rascal."

She invited him to have supper with her one evening, and a week or two later they made arrangements with the church elder to come and marry them.

Ben wasted no time in settling in. One week after the wedding, he started making the changes he felt necessary now that he was going to be a full-time farmer, unlike the late Erasmus. Ben believed that the women could take care of the small stock themselves; besides, he reckoned a little more activity might be the right remedy for his wife's moodiness. But he wasn't going to announce this belief, of course. He would get rid of all the extra hands, and the rest would follow.

Because young Augus spoke Dutch so well, he was the first to go; all the farmers were eager to have him. A *smous* temporarily based in Boshoek took him in exchange for a planter with a missing wheel. For a single calf, old Meneer Venter from the farm next door bought both April and one of the older men. Ben kept Sara and Maria to make sure that his wife would be well taken care of – not forgetting his own lusty needs, which a mature and sickly woman like Tina might find too much to cope with.

April was only too happy to transfer to Meneer Venter's. He'd heard good reports about the farm, and eagerly gathered his few belongings three days before he was due to leave, setting off for his new life without so much as a backward glance.

7

APRIL

Ten years on the Venters' farm and I'll be going on the how-manieth trip to Rustenburg with the oubaas? How these years have flown compared with the three I spent on the Erasmus farm. Don't misunderstand me. I'm not saying that the Venters' farm is my favourite place; I'm talking in comparison. There is only one favourite place for me, and that's my home in Moletji. But then again, I've been away for such a long time that sometimes I think these good feelings I have about it are just lies. My memory of my village is all so dim and vague. But I don't care, as long as my heart still feels good about it, so it will be.

Old Stephanus Venter has been good to me, but I'm saying this again in comparison to what my friends tell me about their bosses. I've learnt since I came here that it's always good to compare things. I've found that just when I think that things with me are quite rotten, I discover a real stink when I talk to other people about their lives. Take Tina Erasmus, for example. She beat us for sport, but there's been very little lashing on the Venters' farm, except when you've done something outrageous like letting the calves suck before milking. Then Oubaas Venter feels forced to act. He administers the first few strokes himself, and then he orders the younger men to take over and finish the job. Depending on who does it, it's usually not too bad. I think Oubaas hurts himself more when he beats us. He is really old.

Oubaas has been spending much more time at home in the past year. His legs are always swollen, so he sits around a lot. To keep himself busy, he decided to teach us to read. Our lessons start just after evening prayers. At first he took on all the farm workers, three boys and two men, but he later dismissed the two men because they made very little progress. I don't know if the same will happen to me too, but one of the men told me that he hated reading because those little letters leapt into his eyes and made them itch when he looked at them for a long time. He said he was happy Oubaas chased him away because his eyes wouldn't itch any more. But I enjoy the lessons, though I can't really say why. Maybe it's just because it's a new thing in my life. Oubaas has the idea that we should be able to read the Bible ourselves. Only two things seem important to the old man these days: teaching his farm folk about God, and going to the church in Rustenburg for *nagmaal* once a month. You would think he's clearing his path to heaven, but I hear he's always been devout. His people also like him very much. Whenever we meet them, they shake his hand so vigorously, I feel a little sorry for him.

Nagmaal Sundays are always special, not only because of the rare chance to leave the farm and meet boys from other farms, but also because you get to know where you stand with Oubaas for the month. Since we learnt how he chooses who accompanies him on the trip to Rustenburg, we try our damnedest to please him, especially before the end of the month. But this does not stop us from feeling worried at the Friday evening prayers before the big announcement. I think Oubaas notices our anxiety, because he drags things on and says the longest prayers, just to torture us. If I'm lucky and I've impressed Oubaas, I'm sometimes chosen.

"April," Oubaas will say more loudly than is necessary, "you will inspan the cart so we can leave early tomorrow morning."

"Ja, Oubaas," I reply, teeth clenched to make sure I show no sign of joy.

And so every month we are judged. The good are separated from the bad, just like we are told it will be on the last day. Careful not to expose myself to anything that will risk the reversal of Oubaas's decision, I always rush to bed before the other boys and cover my head.

We usually leave the farm on Saturday morning, just after milking, and drive briskly so that we will be halfway, passing through the Boshoek farms, by midday. This gives us time enough to reach Rustenburg before sunset. Oubaas prefers to drive the mules himself. And doesn't he just! Because I sit at the back of the wagon behind their seat, I face where we come from and I watch the road slip past very fast. This usually turns my liver upside-down, so that I spend the entire trip trying to hold in the contents of my stomach. I never accept the piece of bread that the missus passes on to me for lunch. But getting there and meeting my friends makes the discomfort worth bearing.

Boys' work begins as soon as we arrive. We offload the carts, take the animals to the stream to drink and then make a fire to prepare supper. Thankfully, Oubaas always arrives much later than everybody else, so we find them already sitting around crackling fires, the air thick with the smoke of roasting meat, and loud voices competing with accordion music. The evenings before *nagmaal* are always festive. Men share *dops* and jokes, while women rock their babies to sleep, quietly soaking up the good atmosphere. A few *dops* later, young men take their wives to dance next to the fire. Oubaas doesn't really approve of this *gedoente*, but he is willing to tolerate it for the occasional company of his old friends.

Meeting with friends who live on other farms is the real advantage of the trip. It gives me a chance to make comparisons, and sometimes the other boys also have useful farming suggestions.

On this particular occasion, however, I found my friend September in a sullen mood. The festivities of the evening seemed only to aggravate his demeanour. It was most unusual behaviour.

"It looks like old Van Wyk has had one *dop* too many, eh!" I remarked, digging my elbow into his side. The sight of the rotund man declaring his love for the moon was sure to take my friend's mind off his woes.

But September did not respond.

"Looks as though we've got a long night ahead of us," I tried.

Still, September did not answer.

"What is it, September?" I asked, trying a more direct tack.

"What?" he replied briskly.

"I asked if you are not well."

Our masters were friends, and they spent time together on these occasions. September and I became friends while we prepared their meals and did jobs for them. He was not much of talker, but today he seemed unusually quiet.

In an uncharacteristically dramatic gesture, he threw down what he was doing and sat down, cupping his head in his hands.

"What's wrong, *broer*?" I asked.

He sighed loudly and said, "One day I'll not be responsible for what I'll do to that Boer."

"Ah," I said knowingly. It was Mostert again.

Mostert was one of those masters who was good for comparison. He made my problems seem small.

"What happened?" I asked.

"I was busy loading the vegetables this morning before we left and he came out fuming from the house, accusing me of something I didn't quite hear. Before I could answer, he slapped me across my face and, as I staggered backwards, he released a right hook that sent me sprawling. I can't take it much longer. I swear, April, I'll kill him."

Mostert was a small but vindictive little man. We often wondered what he would do if September retaliated.

"Mmm," I mused, "I suppose he feels he owns you like his horse."

"Well, even a horse can throw you off," September seethed.

I felt sorry for my friend. He's normally good company, always laughing at every little thing I say. I had observed that things were rather difficult between him and his master. I needed to find something comforting to talk about to take his mind off his worries. Memories from home usually worked. And then it struck me that I did not really know much about September. Where did he come from? We were always chatting and laughing together, but only about things that had happened recently.

Our fire was burning strongly. I sat down next to my friend and told him about a strange recurrent dream I had had the other night. I dreamt that I was back home in Moletji, playing with my younger brother under the thorn tree while my mother was busy working in the field with her friends. We were pushing a stone back and forth to the thudding rhythm of my mother's hoe. Suddenly my mother screamed, "Snake!" and the women scattered in fear. My mother then burst out laughing.

"You cowards," she said. "There's no snake here."

"She was like that, my mother – always liked to tease," I explained to September. "But what was strange was that when the women went back to resume their work, my mother was nowhere to be found. I do miss her still."

"What was your mother like?" I asked, hoping that my story would bring him out of himself. I thought that talking about his past might just be the diversion he needed, but there was also the risk that it might throw up some forgotten pain.

"I never knew my mother," September said. "She died just after I was born."

"Oh," I said.

So much for my attempt to cheer him up, I thought. But I was now too curious to stop.

"Don't worry, my mother's friend who brought me up told me about her," he said. "Sometimes I feel like I really knew her. I also like talking about her, just so that I don't ever forget."

"Well, then, what was she like?"

"Let me see if I can remember ..." September began, and in no time at all he'd lost himself in reverie: "She was slender and tall like a river reed, with strong white teeth that dazzled against her ebony skin when she smiled. She sang and danced like she was created for it. Her fine graceful movements, swaying like branches of a young willow, filled her friends with envy and inflamed young men's hearts. Without her, no feast in the village was worth the trouble."

It was not often that September lost himself in words.

"*Hede*! Was she really like that?" I teased.

September just smiled, leaning back and resting his body on his elbows. He closed his eyes for a while, perhaps wallowing in the feeling his mother's image evoked. Indeed, from where I was sitting, I could see he'd lost a lot of the tension that he had before.

As I'm wont, my mind quickly jumped to comparisons. I took September and put him next to his mother in my mind's eye. Hmm ... the resemblance was a little difficult. September's skin wasn't dark at all – more brown like burnt amber. His hair had a lazy weave that would be out of place on his mother's head. I doubted my friend's ability to sing, but I liked him enough to feel that some of his mother's sunrays had made a home in him: he too was tall and had good teeth.

I thought I should ask him about his father, but decided not to risk anything that might rouse him from his present mood. Instead, I stoked the fire and told him about myself – how the Boers had attacked our village and captured us. Unlike September, images of horror accompanied my reminiscence – my father and brother falling on that bloody night. I wondered about my mother. What became of her? Did she survive? Was she still alive? I remembered my father saying to us so often in the evenings, when he returned from the *kgotla*, that the aches in his knees were beginning to announce that his forefathers were preparing a seat for him. But we all expected that it would be a good while longer before the rest of his body shouted out his departure. In my village, sudden deaths were for young, reckless men ...

My spirits were beginning to sag, so I jumped to my feet to pull myself off this path to unhappiness, and thanked God for a busy life on the farm, which left me with very little time to remember.

8

The church service went on longer than usual, and the boys had to restart the fire twice before the masters began to trickle out of the building.

Visiting Dominee van der Hoff's sermon was a vitriolic attack on the continued subservience to the Cape Synod, which he claimed did not care for the needs of the Transvaal Boers. He poured scorn and ridicule on the mentality of Boers who would risk life and limb to get away from the rule of the Cape and yet continue to entrust their spiritual life to the self-satisfied men of the Synod.

Almost jumping up and down on the pulpit, Van der Hoff had belted out his sermon:

"My dear brothers in Christ, if you did not feel and see God lift and guide your wagons through the deep gorges and passes of the Cape mountains, then something is really wrong with you. It means that your strength and ruggedness are only superficial. Deep down, you are desperate babies clinging to the drying breasts of the Cape Synod. I understand the Synod itself is aware of your *klam* disposition. They are planning the ultimate insult: a spit in your faces. They plan on bringing missionaries from Europe to preach to the black heathens around you when they would not heed your own request for preachers."

"*Hoor, hoor!*" one section of the congregation shouted.

A group near the back started muttering among themselves: "What the hell does this man mean? Who is he? What gives him the right to tell us how to live our lives?"

The church was split right down the middle on this issue. Some influential Boers, such as Kruger, could not agree more with Van der Hoff. They did not see the sense of the lingering dependence of their church on the Cape Synod after all their struggles in the trek. Others, like Venter, believed that spiritual allegiance was not determined by geography, but by conviction of the basic tenets of the church. They also felt that this link to the Cape church provided some continuity against the maelstrom of change that accompanied their relocation.

While the masters were trying to determine their spiritual futures, April and September had more time to talk about important things in their lives. September, noticing April's sadness, said, "You know, one old man I met in the Cape where I once worked told me that the law of the Boer Republic says *inboekselings* can be freed as soon as they reach the age of twenty-five. Did you know that?"

"No."

"I've heard of it more than once and I think it's true."

"What if it's true?"

"I have been on the farms for such a long time and have suffered enough *stront* to think of following up this law, or I'm just going to run away. I think it's time to leave."

"Go on."

"I would like to have my own place and decide things for myself. I'm old enough. I plan to tell my master soon that I want to leave. What about you?" September asked.

"I don't think we are far apart age-wise. I'm sure it's time for me too, but I haven't really thought about my future. But, if there's a legal way to do it, I'd like to try it," April replied.

"With that bastard Mostert, I know it won't be easy, but I'll be damned if I don't try."

"You know," April responded, "when I do get to leave, my first task will be to look for my sister. I last saw her on the day we were booked. I hear some of the children from my village were given to farmers in Potchefstroom. I've never been to this town, but I suspect that is where I'll find my sister."

"I'm not quite sure what I'll do when I leave," September replied. "Before I came here I worked for a *smous*, and we used to travel to the Cape to fetch goods to sell. We were always on the road with no rest at all, and I came to hate that kind of vagabond life. I want to settle down and make a life of my own."

"Maybe you could come along and help me find my sister first."

"That's fine. We could do casual jobs on different farms to make money as we make our way there, but first we must make plans to leave the farms we live on now."

9

Oubaas Venter was a worried man. Clouds of civil war were fast gathering in the Transvaal. The split over the continued links with the Cape Synod was fuelled by another quarrel on the political front. The Boers of the Transvaal Republic could not agree on who was to be their leader. Schoeman and Pretorius were vying for the position, and each had formed supporting bands that were ready to take up arms to defend their interests. Recently, these two bands had been seen exchanging fisticuffs in Potchefstroom, and even shots across the Highveld. This skirmish between brothers left ordinary Boers such as Venter perplexed and astonished at the trekkers' self-destructiveness. They simply could not believe that their hard-won freedom could be sacrificed to such foolish quarrels. Worse still was the fact that it was increasingly difficult not to take sides. Even church services were sometimes interrupted by brawls.

The Venters felt that they could no longer endure this unstable life, especially alone on a farm at their age. They decided to go and live on their son's farm along the Crocodile River, near Pretoria. They would then at least be assured of help if things took a turn for the worse. The decision seemed correct as far as their safety was concerned, but the question of what would happen to their farm folk stuck in their throats like a piece of half-chewed biltong. The Venters saw themselves as the moral parents of the *inboekselings*, and they believed that their servants thought as much of them. For a whole week they prayed and wrestled over what was to become of each of their servants.

Finally, they came up with two plans. The first was that their absence would be brief, and that they would install one of the new arrivals in Rustenburg as a caretaker so that things would continue as normal for their folk. But they doubted it was realistic to think that they would return to farming at their age. The second plan, for a permanent departure, sounded more reasonable, but was more difficult to accept. They would distribute the younger boys to their neighbours, and April, who was now a strapping youth, could perhaps be interested in life as a free man, just like Isaiah who had recently been freed from Herklaas Malan's farm to go and live in Moruleng. They could set him up with a few head of cattle and sheep to make a life for himself in the village.

They enquired about their neighbour Visagie's willingness to take on the younger boys, and he agreed. And so the second plan was adopted.

Oubaas Venter decided to make the announcement at their Sunday service, building up to the news with a reading from Hebrews 11, verse 24:

"It was faith that made Moses, when he had grown up, refuse to be called the son of the king's daughter!" Venter bellowed. "He preferred to suffer with God's people rather than to enjoy sin for a little while."

At this sentiment, Oubaas paused and examined each servant's face staring back at him. He cleared his throat and continued.

"He reckoned that to suffer scorn for the Messiah was worth far more than all the treasures of Egypt, for he kept his eyes on a future reward."

Oubaas gestured towards the church exit, and the listeners' gaze followed inquisitively towards this envisioned future.

"A test of faith calls for a strong response that looks beyond the circumstances," he explained later in his sermon. "What we are called to do may hurt us in the short term, but in faith we should trust that God will always do what's good for us."

By this time, the farm folk felt sure that some terrible fate was about to strike, but Oubaas went on to explain the need for their departure and the arrangements he'd made for the younger boys. He paused for a while, not quite sure of how his next statement would land, but after a while he said that he was not going to make any arrangements for April, because he was old enough to decide where he wanted to go.

Touched by this wonderful coincidence, April assured his master that nothing was in vain, especially his reading lessons. It was all part of the master plan. Slowly, he read through Matthew 19, verse 4:

"Jesus answered, 'Haven't you read the scripture that says that in the beginning the Creator made people male and female?' And God said, 'For this reason a man will leave his father and mother and unite with his wife, and the two will become one.'"

Well, what do you know? When and where did April meet this young woman? Oubaas wondered, shocked but pleased at this romantic twist of fate.

10

APRIL

I couldn't believe how swiftly Oubaas moved into action to clear the farm, but what really dropped my jaw were my parting gifts – a heifer and a young bull.

I found Oubaas having breakfast with the ou missus as usual when I brought the milk in from the kraal. I noticed the two animals outside, but so much was changing on the farm that I didn't think too much of them.

Then Oubaas called me to the *voorhuis* and said in his pre-*nagmaal* tone: "April, you've been with us a long time and you've been very good."

Oh, Lord, I thought, *I hope he's not thinking of taking me with him*.

"I agree with what you said last night, April," Oubaas continued. "A man of your age should have his own family. I've decided to give you those two animals you saw outside to start you off in life. You can decide where you want to go and live."

Then the missus interrupted: "That little heifer is actually pregnant, April. May it signal many young Aprils soon," she said, giving me a knowing smile.

Talk about knocking me down with a feather, an old woman could have blown me away with her breath. Me: owner of two cattle, on the way to a life of fruitful multiplication! Though this was not really my idea of a new life, I fell on my knees and thanked my master profusely.

"You've been like parents to me. How will I live without you?" I lamented.

"*Kom nou*, April," Oubaas said impatiently. "You are a big man now."

"Yes, Oubaas," I said, pulling myself together, "I will join Isaiah in Moruleng. Is tomorrow acceptable?"

I would indeed go and find Isaiah, but not to stay. I had other plans. I would ask him to keep my animals while I found September and we set our own future in motion. I knew Isaiah would be pleased to keep my cattle. He was well settled in the village of Moruleng with a wife and seven children.

I decided to leave the Venters' farm early the next morning after my worst night ever. I couldn't sleep for most of it, with my mind racing around like a hungry boar:

What if I fail to adjust ... can't feed myself ... things get worse instead of better?

But I'm young and strong; I've survived a lot. I'm ...

What will I do without Oubaas?

I'm old enough ...

Finally the mental struggle wore me down and I fell asleep. I woke up with a start at the first cock crow and quickly pulled on my trousers. I put on the new *velskoene* that Oubaas had allowed me to make from the leather that was left over after I'd made him a pair. I didn't like wearing shoes much, but I thought I should on this special occasion. I threw on the shirt the old man had given me when we first started going to Rustenburg. Everything I owned was either on my body or in my little sack. I nearly forgot my *karos*, which was still on the floor where I slept. I rolled it up and tied it to my herding stick. With my bundle slung over my shoulder, I stepped for the very last time out of the hut that had contained me for so many years.

Ah, leave it open for the poor wretch who'll follow, I said to myself as I walked through the door.

I went past the main house to pick up the provisions that the missus had offered me the night before and then proceeded to fetch my animals, the beginning of my wealth.

"*Kom, kom, Swartland, Lady Nooi*, on your feet!" I shouted as I drove them briskly to the farm gate.

I should give these animals my own names, not leftovers from the Venters' farm, I decided. New life, new everything!

I stepped up my pace, almost breaking into a trot. A creeping exhilaration rose from the pit of my stomach, up my throat and exploded in a wild scream. I leapt into the air and erupted into loud hyena-like laughter, which travelled all the way to the Venters' dogs' ears. They barked furiously, as if to suppress me. My cattle were also startled by the noise, so I called myself to order.

But I was free.

I decided not to think too much about this new state of freedom in case it turned out to be a disappointment. Instead, I made my way to Moruleng in earnest, letting the many thoughts that crowded my mind fight for entry.

11

MAJA

I arrived in Moruleng just before sunset, and all the familiar sights and sounds came rushing to meet me: red dust mingling with smoke from the evening fires; women balancing pots of water on their heads; slim black pigs scurrying around, picking up bits of discarded porridge and waving their short tails to the tune of their high-pitched grunts; and the sing-song voices of herd boys leaping over the rest to coax their animals into the kraal entrances.

So much like home, I said to myself, almost overwhelmed by the memory and sudden realisation of all that I'd missed.

A voice from within then said, *Forget about all this travel you are thinking about and settle down next to Isaiah, just like you promised Oubaas.*

But my heart retreated and reminded me that I'd spent all those years on the Venters' farm, only going to Rustenburg occasionally. If I was to be my own boss, it should show. I should test this freedom, stretch it and pin it down like a piece of leather to be tanned. Then I'd settle down. Besides, there's my sister: I had to go and find her.

I found Isaiah tanning leather in his backyard. He'd heard via various sources of my release and had been expecting me. It did not take too much to convince him to keep the animals. His eldest son was just about to marry, and my cattle would provide him with good start-up stock.

Were it not for Isaiah's Dutch, which he spoke most of the time, he would be just like any other Mokgatla man. His *inboekseling* past was far in the distance, and his Lesotho origin was a forgotten dream.

Isaiah had come to the Transvaal by sheer accident. He'd been only a small boy of about ten years of age when a French *smous*, who used to visit the French missionaries in Morija, asked for Isaiah to accompany him on a short trip to the Transvaal, promising to return him to his village. His father agreed because he trusted the missionaries, but Isaiah never saw his family again. The French man, De Villiers, met a Boer damsel, fell stupidly in love and forgot all about his promise to Isaiah's father. De Villiers decided to make his life in the Transvaal, where Isaiah worked for him for a while, but he soon decided to move to Natal. Because he wanted to travel light, he shed Isaiah. He sold him to Herklaas Malan in return for a horse cart. So Isaiah worked on the farm for most of his youth, until Malan's children gave him his freedom when their father died suddenly during a hunt.

We sat up late into the night talking about life in the village, how people still saw Isaiah and his family as foreigners – even after so many years and his sons marrying local girls. I wasn't surprised, because Isaiah had built his house on the outskirts of the village, as if to acknowledge his foreigner status. He said he preferred living apart like this because it was "safest". I did not ask him what he felt safe from. As it was such a balmy night, we took our mats outside and slept in the courtyard.

I got up very early the next morning and tip-toed off to get myself ready to go. Isaiah's wife had left a couple of sticks of biltong and cold *pap* for me to take as provisions. One of his boys had kindly dropped his *sebinjolo* next to the food to keep me busy on my long way to Boshoek.

My plan for the day was a loose one, but I would pace myself to reach Boshoek in the evening. I knew it would take a day or so to find September. It might even be necessary for me to find a job on the farms there to get closer to the people so I could gather information about him. I would do whatever it took.

The morning was still, except for the rustling sound I made as I walked through the tall grass. Hares darted out of my way, and now and again a larger animal hissed past. In the distance I heard the roar of their king, so I decided to sing and make a noise to scare them all off. The first song that came to my mind was a hymn that we sang at evening prayers with Oubaas.

No, no, not that! I shouted. I wanted to sing a song of brave men – what my father and his regiment would have sung as they entered the village dragging their victim buffalo. I strummed the little *sebinjolo* to remind myself. The tune was clear enough, but there were no words. It was too long ago. I decided to make up my own words and I sang at the top of my lungs.

As my song spiralled up, so did my thoughts. I decided I needed to make a few changes. First, my name ... There was absolutely no need to carry around this Boer name. My parents had given me a name by which my ancestors recognised me. If I'm free, then I should present myself to them appropriately. Maja is my name. *Maja a sekete sa boopelo.*

A contrary thought then advised, *but you won't get a job with a name like that.*

In the end I decided the Boers could call me what they liked, but I would be Maja to everyone else.

I then changed my mind about reaching Boshoek the same day, just to give myself a little time to get used to being in charge. I slowed down my pace and really worked on my *sebinjolo*, trying out as many songs as I could remember. I struggled, but now and again I hit one that I could complete.

By midday I was halfway to my destination. I sought a large morula tree to relax under, eating my lunch in its cool shade. When I finished eating, I lay back python-style and let my stomach do its work.

A couple of large drops of rain rudely roused me from my long nap. The sky was dark with rain clouds and lightning flashed all around, promising a heavy downpour. I migrated to a thicker grove of karee trees, and wove myself a hammock with their long thin branches, where I would spend the night.

I woke up to a bright blue sky, so innocent-looking you wouldn't think it was responsible for my wet blanket and clothes. I shook them out and hung them up to dry while I kindled a fire to make the last bit of coffee that the missus had given me.

Immediately thereafter I was on my way to Boshoek. I headed straight for Commissioner Kruger's farm. I'd heard he was taking on people to dig out trees from an area where he wanted to plant a mielie field. I hoped to work there long enough to track down September and collect provisions for the next leg of my journey to find my long-lost sister.

12

MAJA

Two weeks into my job on Kruger's farm, one of the men told me that he'd heard that September had already left Mostert's and was living somewhere around Rustenburg.

"Good," I said, "at least he got away."

In spite of my eagerness to find my friend, I decided it was prudent to continue with the job until I was given my rations at the end of the month before going off to look for him.

At the end of what seemed like an endless month, I left Kruger's farm quite unceremoniously and headed for the fresh produce market, where most of the men wanting work loitered. It was known as an excellent source of information and I was sure to find out more about September.

I arrived around midday and settled myself under a nearby tree to watch the men work. There were six of them offloading vegetables from a wagon. I was hoping to spot my friend, but he wasn't there. At the sound of a whistle, the men dropped their work and came to sit under my tree. The man next to me unwrapped his food parcel and started eating an unaccompanied piece of *pap*. I saw an entry into my enquiry, and broke a piece of biltong from my pack to give to him.

"Dry *pap* is a mighty job to contend with," I said, offering him the piece.

"Thank you," he replied. "Don't they say that even dogs face it with disgust?"

Taking periodic bites from the biltong, the man attacked his *pap* with a little more gusto. When he finished, he leant back and lay down for a short nap. I joined him and lay back too, but instead of closing my eyes to sleep, I explained my mission.

"I wonder if you can help me," I enquired. "I'm looking for a friend of mine who used to work in Boshoek. I understand he's living around Rustenburg somewhere and might be working here at the market. Have you ever seen him?"

The man did not respond and, remembering my manners, I started again, "Let me introduce myself first. I am Maja, son of Moloto, originally from the faraway land of Bapedi, but I have lived around these parts for a long time now."

"*Dumela morwarra.* Greetings," the man said. "I am Mogami from the land of Batlhako. But tell me, my brother, of all the men here, how would I know which one is your friend?"

"My friend is different," I said. "Not dark like you and me. He's like a half and half ... you understand?"

"Half and half ... ?" he mused, and went quiet for a while. Then he nodded and said, "There's a man like that who comes here to help now and again. He arrives, does his bit to get rations for the day and disappears just like that."

"Is this man tall and strong?" I asked excitedly.

"That's him. He almost landed us in trouble when he first came because he used to lift two bags for every one we lifted. The Boers started thinking we were very lazy. But I don't know when he'll be here again. You'll have to keep coming here to check. Maybe you'll bump into him one day."

Frustrating as it was, this seemed like the most sensible option. I decided to help the men just to while away the time. I was also hoping they would offer me a place to sleep. While we were busy with our work, a strange young white couple approached the foreman to buy some vegetables. Mogami nudged me to watch them.

"This is an unusual pair," he said. "They come here every other day to pick up this or that, and the woman always follows the man around. People laugh at them because they cannot understand when the man finds time to do work with his wife traipsing after him like that."

"Where do they come from?" I asked.

"No one knows," Mogami replied, "but look at them! Just look at their clothes."

It was a truly bizarre display. The man seemed to have fashioned himself after a crow. He wore a black suit and a white shirt with a high collar that clung to his throat. His hair was yellow, like *tamboekie* grass – I think from all the time he spent in the sun. The woman, on the other hand, had brown hair, but they both had eyes so blue, you wouldn't think they could see. She, too, wore dark-coloured clothes, and her top had a white lacy collar that also reached high up her neck. Her skirt was long and big, like a tent. It swept the ground as she walked, creating a small cloud of dust, which finally settled on the lower part of her dress, giving it a motley red-brown hue. Because she was short, the big skirt made her look plump, like a well-fed chicken, quite incongruous with her pretty young face. Her shoes were hard to imagine, but the permanent grimace on her face seemed to indicate some form of discomfort in the region of her feet.

"Why would a man want his wife to dress like that?" I said. "In this heat, too!"

"I think he's lost his mind," Mogami chuckled. "That's why he hasn't got a horse and spends his days going around in circles. The man doesn't even have a hat!"

By this time all the men were watching the couple. One of them then said, "I think poverty sits badly on a white man. It makes him do strange things, like wearing a shirt that could strangle him any minute."

We all burst out laughing, our curiosity about the strange couple now satisfied, and continued with our work.

I went home with the men and came back the next morning, still hoping that September would be there, but he wasn't. I was beginning to worry that I would never find him. Then one of the men said that he'd heard that my friend had taken a ride to Potchefstroom with a *smous* who bought supplies there. He told them that he was going to join a friend who was there to look for his sister.

"*My gonnas*! What a mess!" I said. "September might already be on his way back and I might just miss him if I try to follow him."

I decided to stay on in Rustenburg and wait for him in the hope that he would hear of my movements. In the meantime, I could help the men at the market in return for food and shelter.

13

MAJA

A week later, the strange couple came back to the market. The woman did not look well at all. She was all flushed and tired. With that dress on, one couldn't be sure, but she looked like she was in the family way.

What a foolish man, I thought.

They bought more goods than usual. The man carried most of it (including the groceries they'd bought earlier), but the woman was going to have to cope with the rest of the produce. I felt sorry for her.

"You have a lot to carry. Do you have far to go?" I shouted from where we were working.

They ignored my question and continued packing their vegetables into bags.

I dropped my load, approached them and asked again: "That's a lot of weight you are carrying there. Will you manage?"

Still they did not answer.

"You could leave some of your things here and we could drop them off at your home when we finish work," I continued.

At last the man acknowledged me: "How will you know where to drop our … our bags; you know not where we are staying," he answered in faltering Dutch.

"A human being has a mouth for a reason," I said. "I can hear you are not from these parts. Where do you come from?"

"We live across the little stream. Over there," the man replied, gesturing towards a small valley. "It's not a long distance on a cool day, but on a hot one like this it is tiring out my wife."

All the more reason to leave her at home, I thought.

"Well, we are new here," the man stammered. "I think we should be going. I can't spend all day here talking to you."

I was surprised by the young man's nervousness. I decided to help them carry their goods; after all, it was already late in the afternoon and we would be finishing work soon.

"*Bakwena*, we don't want the woman dying in front of our eyes!" I shouted to my friends. "I will join you later at the camp."

The men laughed and waved me off. I picked up the couple's bags, and though they were a little hesitant to accept my help, they eventually gave in.

"Where did you learn to speak Dutch so well?" the young man asked while we walked.

"Here and there," I replied. "I've lived in these parts a long time."

The man introduced himself as Henri Gonin and his wife as Jenny. They told me that they had come from Switzerland a year ago, to start what he called "missionary work among the natives".

I nearly introduced myself as April, but then remembered I wasn't looking for a job. How could I? This man was even poorer than I was. So I introduced myself as Maja and explained my history briefly.

"Tell me, what kind of work is missionary work?" I asked.

"It is the preaching and teaching to people about Christ," Gonin answered.

"Isn't your country very far from here?"

"I crossed oceans on a ship to get here," Gonin replied.

This struck me as nonsensical: "Couldn't you do this work in your own country?" I asked. "I know about Christ. My old boss taught us about him in his house; although sometimes he came to Rustenburg for church services, but he really did it himself on his own farm. I don't understand why you had to leave your country for this work."

"The Bible calls us to spread the Word of God to all people," Gonin explained.

"Are you saying there are no people in your part of the world to whom you could spread the Word?"

"The need is greater here," Gonin stated resolutely.

"How do you know that?" I responded. "I told you: our baas taught us about Christ, and you are telling me the need is greater here. Who needs it? Anyway, have you succeeded in spreading the Word?"

"No, I haven't," Gonin said, dropping his head. "I have hardly started."

"That's what I thought," I said. "And you risked being swallowed by the big fish of the ocean for that?"

I thought the man was stark-raving crazy. At this point we reached their house. I put their parcels next to the door and bade them farewell.

"Wait," Gonin said, "Please stay with us for supper."

"What?" I said. "Stay for supper with you?" I was now certain that things were not well here.

"Yes, please," Jenny said, holding out her hands. "We have not been making friends with people here. You are the first one who's ... who's ..." She sighed at her inability to find the right words.

I agreed to stay, as long as I could leave to join my friends at the market before it got too late. These people were definitely strange, but I was intrigued to hear more of their story.

Gonin invited me to take a seat at the table with him while his wife was preparing the supper.

"I see why you find what I'm saying strange," he said, settling into his chair. "It makes no sense to take all these risks only to come and fail at what I came for."

"Mmm. You can say that again ..." I replied.

"But I can assure you, it's not for not trying," Gonin interrupted. "I want to start my mission in one of the villages here, in these parts, but the Transvaal government has been very difficult."

"I'm not surprised," I said. "I'm sure, like me, they don't understand what you are about."

He ignored what I'd said, and continued with his woes: "I don't know what they want. When we came first to the Transvaal, we went straight to Landdrost Steyn in Potchefstroom to get permission for our work. My church council in the Cape has also been trying very hard to make it right for us with them."

He rose from the table and fetched a pile of letters from his bag. It was clearly the first time he'd been able to share his frustration with another person, and he was eager to plead his case.

"Look at all these letters ..." he lamented, pouring a pile of papers onto the table. He held up the latest from Landdrost Steyn and read it.

He pulled out another letter, wailing, "Just look now at this: the Cape Synod is even writing to the Council of the Synod of the Transvaal Hervormde Kerk to get us help. Look!"

Gonin went on and read the letter without waiting for my response.

4 June 1862

Dear Brothers in Christ,

I'm writing to you with the firm belief that as Christians we are committed to spreading the Word of God to all corners of the world. I hereby request the help from the council of the Hervormde Kerk for the preachers that were sent out as missionaries during this year by the Nederduitse Church to work under the heathen in the Transvaal, as much as possible to advance their worthy attempts.

Yours in the name of our Lord,
L. Neethling
Secretary
Cape Synod.

"But look at how they responded," he said, holding up a short letter from Landdrost Steyn, dated 23rd May 1862, and reading:

Honourable Gentlemen,

The law of the Transvaal has been fully explained to yourselves and I hope you understand. I must emphasise that there will not be the least commotion, as your honour will have to blame yourself for the consequences.

Faithfully,
Landdrost Steyn.

"It is really amazing," Gonin sighed. "I don't understand why the landdrost can't see how unjust they are. You see, they think that we are just a front for the British government to influence the natives against them. Why? Why would we want to do that?"

"This is exactly what I thought," I said irritably, when he'd finished. "You said the need was greater here. How can it be so when no one, not even the government of the Transvaal, agrees? Shouldn't you have made sure that you were wanted before you left your country?"

"It is not so easy," Gonin explained. "We are Christians, and so is the Transvaal government. We both believe in what the Bible is saying: preach the gospel to all people. But what we don't agree on is the natives, and whether 'all people' includes natives."

"Still my point," I said. "Why didn't you check?"

Jenny brought the food and, after she had said grace, I said politely to Gonin, "If I may say so, I suggest you go back home. You've obviously made a mistake."

Gonin did not answer. He attacked his food rather fiercely, and in between large mouthfuls repeated, "You don't understand, you really don't understand."

Because it was already late in the night, I agreed to sleep in the *buitekamer*, and in the morning Gonin offered me a place to stay until September came back, in return for help in the garden.

14

As usual, Gonin and Maja met in the garden at sunrise. Already Maja was carrying two buckets of water from the well, every muscle on his lean shirtless torso rippling as he moved. Maja was tall and well built, with muscles so tightly packed together, they left no room for any fat. He met Gonin with a hearty greeting every morning, but today it was muted and Gonin couldn't help but notice.

"Are you well?" he asked.

"I'm fine," Maja replied curtly. "I hope you are well too."

At a loss on how to proceed, Gonin picked up his shovel, and they worked in this unusual silence. Although Maja had agreed to stay on with the Gonins, he had spent a sleepless night wrestling with a situation that seemed to be entrapping him. His vow to make a free life for himself haunted him. He had decided to leave, but was struggling with going back on his word.

"You know," Gonin said at last, "I've done all that I can to start my mission, but I have not been successful. I would give it up … stop … if only it wouldn't be such an abomination to the Lord. I don't know what else to do."

He paused for Maja's response, but none came.

"I know this is not your problem," Gonin continued, "but I need all the support I can get. I've talked to all the big people, even Kruger, but nothing changes. He's encouraging, but makes no big decisions. He's worried to look like he supports us because of this war that's coming. It's made them all cautious in helping us."

"I'm sorry to say, but the problem is of your making," Maja replied.

"What shall I do?" Gonin asked desperately.

"Go home. Or find another chief who'll have you," Maja suggested distractedly.

"Ah, this is good advice," Gonin said. "I'm hoping to go and speak to Chief Kgamanyane, but I'm not sure if he's come back from the hunt for the elephants."

"Well, let's go and find out," Maja responded, and, seeing the opportunity to deliver his bad news on the tail end of his offer to help, he announced, "I'm leaving soon. I have to go and find my sister."

"I understand, but I appreciate your coming with me," Gonin said. "Anything that we can do will be much better than this ... this ... uncertainty. I'll ask for horses from Mr Teens, so we can ride to Moruleng tomorrow morning."

The two men set off very early the next morning, and Jenny stayed at home alone. She decided to lie in bed until late because she got tired so easily these days, and her back hurt a lot with any form of exertion. Their little house was really just one room, which they had subdivided by means of a curtain so that they could have a living and sleeping area. Only one small window provided ventilation. By ten o'clock it was oven-hot, and so Jenny decided to get up and make herself a late breakfast. She hauled herself up and swung her legs to the floor. Her feet had hardly landed when a hot pain tore through her side and crawled across her lower back to the other side. She clung to the bedding as beads of sweat rolled down her forehead. She waited for a second stab, but it did not come.

Phew, what was that? Jenny thought that she had probably been too rough getting up. She crossed to the living room and pumped the Primus stove to make tea. Last night's dishes and Henri's shirts, which she had soaked, stared at her from the corner, all unwashed.

If only Henri could help a little more in the house. I know he's a good man, but I'm finding it quite difficult to cook and do all the washing up in the evenings.

I shouldn't complain so much. Washing up hardly takes a minute. I'll just start with the dishes before I make tea.

Jenny reached across to pick up the kettle from the Primus stove, and another bolt of pain shot through her back, burning her kidneys and spine as it moved. She whimpered. Her lower back seemed to be splitting away from the rest of her. She sat down holding her tummy, worried that the violence in her body might kill the baby. She was now certain that there was more to these pains than getting up recklessly. She had read a bit about childbirth, and she expected contractions to herald the baby, but they were supposed to start in front, just below her navel – at least that's what the book said.

Could this be the onset of a miscarriage? No, miscarriages happen earlier in pregnancy. Could these be the beginning of the real thing?

She went back to the bedroom to consult her trusted motherhood manual. Yes, it said, sometimes labour can start as severe back pain. She pulled out the notes that she and Gonin had worked out to outline what they should do as labour began. The process was clearly laid out, step by step:

1. *Stay active in the early stages.*
2. *Time the contractions.*
3. *Breathe deeply during a contraction and breathe out slowly when it has passed.*
4. *Lie down as the contractions get stronger and more frequent (the husband can administer a back massage).*
5. *Call the midwife, heat water and prepare the bed for birth.*

Jenny decided to be active: make tea, wash the dishes and then Henri's shirts. She was just about to pour her second cup when the same arrow of pain cut through her back again. This time her tummy tightened as the pain moved across. *These are contractions indeed*, Jenny thought. *It's been twenty minutes since the last one.*

She took a chair outside in the sun and put down the tub containing Henri's shirts to wash them, hoping that the warmth of the sun would ease the contractions. She rubbed the collars, the sleeves and the body of the shirts with a kind of energy she had not felt in a long time. Her body was fighting back, and slowly her mood changed. She felt buoyed and convinced that she had what it takes to get through this encounter. Bending down to rinse the shirt she had just finished washing, the pain suddenly contradicted her newly found confidence. She clung to the tub and puffed until it passed.

Well, it takes twenty minutes to wash a shirt clean, Jenny thought bravely.

She washed the next shirt and waited for the contraction. It came on time. Jenny filled her lungs with air as the pain walked through her back. She proceeded to the next shirt, and waited. It did not disappoint; it came on time, like its predecessors. By the time she was ready to hang out the shirts, Jenny noticed that the pains took a little less than twenty minutes to come. She hung out the shirts to dry and removed the tub from the chair, flopping down on it to wait for the total onslaught.

Breathe in and breathe out! she coaxed herself, but her energy was slowly seeping away and a clammy kind of depression crept in to replace it. A fly settled on her nose, but Jenny left it. It crawled up her forehead and waded through the pool of sweat that had formed. The fly seemed not to enjoy the swim, because it flew away of its own accord.

Jenny started to feel too hot in the sun, but she was afraid to go inside and be truly alone. She gave in to the pain. Sobs took over from her controlled breathing. The contractions ignored her misery and continued unabated, coming closer and closer to one another.

"Mommy, mommy!" the woman cried. "Oh, Lord! Was this part of Your plan? That I should have my baby alone? In this wretched land? What good would that do to anyone? What good in the big scheme of things? Lord, please bring Henri back soon. I can't bear this, it's so painful!"

Jenny dragged herself up to go and lie down. She let the pain take its course. Too weary to continue watching her body suffer, she allowed her mind to escape, to inspect the evening instead. A soft shaft of light from the departing sun peeped through the cracks in the door. Moths skipped in and out of the line of light, like girls on a skipping rope. The neighbourhood dogs sounded agitated. They barked and bayed in alternating crescendos. Younger dogs seemed to lead the chorus. As if to claim their audience, the crickets chirped louder than usual. Suddenly the sound of approaching horses intruded upon all the other sounds, and happiness welled in Jenny's heart. Henri was back. She wiped away her tears and tried to pull herself together, forcing herself up to let her husband in. Just one step from the bed, and something popped in her lower abdomen. A warm liquid gushed down her legs to the floor. Jenny let out a blood-curdling scream.

"What's that?" Henri said, latching his horse to the fence. "I think that was Jenny screaming."

He ran into the house and found Jenny slumped over the bed with a wet slippery patch at her knees. He picked her up and laid her on the bed.

"The baby's coming, Henri," she gasped. "Call Mrs Moolman, quickly. Quickly!"

"Are you sure, Jenny?" Gonin asked, trying to take in the news. "Where are the notes? Let me give you a back rub."

Jenny yelled again as another contraction ploughed through her. There was clearly no time for back rubs. Henri jumped up to go and call the midwife.

Mevrou Moolman was sitting on the stoep enjoying a cherished cup of coffee. She had just come back from Hettie Steenkamp's home, where she had delivered a baby girl. Her mule cart was still standing inspanned in front of the house. Her long experience had taught her never to be hasty to outspan when she came back from a baby's birth; human babies had a secret pact never to arrive alone on this earth.

Mevrou Moolman poured her second cup, her movements deliberate and attuned over the years to the babies' slow arrival. Wherever possible she conserved her energy, never rushing around, so as to cope with three or four deliveries a night. She was the only midwife in Rustenburg and was overworked, especially with the Boers taking the injunction to be fruitful and multiply so seriously.

True to the rule, a figure appeared across the river. Gonin was approaching Mevrou Moolman's house with the long strides so typical of a distressed young husband. She gulped down her coffee and went inside to get her bag ready. She came out to find him fumbling with the latch of her normally easy-to-open gate.

"*Toemaar, toemaar,*" said Mevrou Moolman, as she locked her door. "Leave that and get on the cart. Where do you live? How long has she been in labour? Has the water broken?"

"What?" replied Gonin agitatedly.

"I said, where do you stay?"

"Yes, there is the broken water," Gonin said. "I think she's been all day in labour. She is having a lot pain. Is that normal?"

"Of course it is," Mevrou Moolman replied. "But first we have to get to her. Where is your house?"

"Turn left at that big morula tree," Gonin answered. "Our house is facing the road straight after the corner."

Shortly thereafter, they arrived at Gonin's house.

"I see you have the water on," Mevrou Moolman said calmly as she entered Jenny's room. "Good, now leave us alone. We'll call you when we are ready."

Gonin and Maja waited just outside the door, but Gonin could not sit down. He paced furiously, trying the door every other minute.

"I think we better go to the garden to rein in your anxiety," Maja suggested. "My people say that a man who carries on like you will cast a nasty spell on the baby."

Maja had been too young when he left his village to have known of any such beliefs, but he had to invent something that would calm Gonin's agitation.

Wide-eyed, Gonin followed Maja to the garden. He picked up a fork and attacked the ground with so much zest that Maja feared they might lose the plants they had tended for so long.

"Be careful!" he shouted through the dust. "We still have to harvest from this crop."

Of all the things that made Gonin homesick, their front door in Rustenburg was first on the list. The scratching noise it made when it opened was to him a practical demonstration of the difference between civilised and uncivilised society. All of a sudden the loathsome sound emerged from his house, and never was hatred so quickly transformed to love. Like a shot, he was out of the garden, stomping on the plants as he ran to the door.

Mevrou Moolman was standing at the door with a bundle wrapped in a white knitted blanket.

"It's a boy," she said, handing the baby to Gonin.

PART II

An upheaval; storm-stern
As the pregnant sky
That'll shed rainfall ...
The mother dies a little
And the child
Cries, a declaration: 'I'm alive!'

MONGANE SEROTE
MOTHER AND CHILD

15

September appeared at the market in Rustenburg just as unexpectedly as he had left. Without even checking to see if he was still welcome, he joined the workmen and started offloading bags of cabbage from the waiting wagons.

Maja had fallen into the routine of making his daily turn at the market at lunch time. He lay under a tree next to Mogami, and as usual they started to chat about this and that. But Maja was not in an overly sociable mood. He was beginning to feel very restless and unhappy about his long wait for September, and the apparent return to the old way of life under white people. After a few minutes of stilted conversation, he shut his eyes to cut out the glare of the midday sun, and in no time he was under a blanket of sleep, hiding from his morbid thoughts.

The back-to-work whistle roused him rudely from his rest. He sat up with a start and, lo and behold, there was September towering over his still-sluggish body.

"Is this what has become of you since you left the Venters?" he boomed from above. "*'n Luislang* that just sleeps and eats?"

"*My vaderland*, who's this before my eyes?" Maja replied. "September, you are the luckiest man alive. I was planning my evening departure as I lay here."

"*Dit lieg jy*. You were sleeping," September laughed.

Maja jumped up and grabbed his friend's hand like a calf's hind-leg. No more words were necessary. Their plans were already too delayed. September had made it halfway to Potchefstroom before deciding to turn back, as he couldn't see himself going through free life without his friend.

The two set off immediately to tell Gonin about their decision to go and find Maja's sister. As they walked, they recounted the events of the past few weeks and plotted their route, deciding to make their way to the Nederduitse Kerk of the local *Oorlams* community of Potchefstroom, a Dutch-speaking community of former *inboekselings*.

But before they left Rustenburg, Maja confronted September about some important terms of their new life, especially the issue of their names. Everyone around Rustenburg used Maja's real name, but his friend didn't seem in the least bit concerned about using the arbitrary title of September.

"I really don't think you should go on using that name," Maja said to him as they were having supper on their last evening in Rustenburg.

September stopped eating and looked up. "Why not?" he asked.

"We should use the names our parents gave us. That will show that we're free men," Maja explained. "So, what name did your mother give you?"

"I don't know," September replied, returning his attention to his meal. "I think you are making a fuss. I don't see why a name should matter, as long as I'm making my own decisions."

"Listen, I'm really serious about this," Maja said, surprised at September's response. "We are not cats and dogs that go by anything the master pleases. Our names tell people where we come from. So, now, what shall we call you?"

"Polomane," September said dismissively. "I was told she named me Polomane after her father, but I've never used the name. It's just part of the legend about my mother."

Maja was satisfied: "That sounds good enough to me. From now on you'll be called Polomane," he declared. "No more September. I hope you'll get used to it, and my new name. I don't want any slips, especially when we are with my sister."

"That fine, if that's what's needed in our new circumstances," September said, glad to put the issue to rest. "It makes no bloody difference to me. Don't be surprised when I don't respond to it at first."

Leaving the Gonins was easy, as the couple was intensely absorbed in their newborn. They saw and heard nothing but the baby. After quickly introducing Polomane and vaguely promising to return, Maja and his friend set off for Potchefstroom. They made no decision about how long they would stay there – as long as it took to find Maja's sister. Polomane was not too averse to staying permanently, because his departure from Mostert's farm had been quite unpleasant.

They reached their destination on Saturday evening. It had taken them a week of walking, running, competing and showing off their stamina. Maja, the leaner, always won, and he gloated thoroughly.

"Sorry I had to put you through this," he said, with a glint in his eye. "A cheetah like me can't always imagine how difficult it is for someone else to keep pace."

"Oh, Apr … sorry, Maja, I see your mouth runs just as fast as you."

"Come, *boet*, it's not that bad," Maja replied patronisingly.

A few miles from Potchefstroom, they met up with two men driving a wagon delivering goods from Pretoria. The men were happy to have different company after so many days together on their trip. Maja and Polomane shared their mission with them, and the men gladly offered them shelter for the night. They also advised them that the church was the most likely place to find anyone in their *lokasie*.

"*Lokasie?* What's that?" Maja asked.

"It's where we live," one of the men answered. "Don't you know?"

"No, I've never heard of a *lokasie* before. Is it the same as a village, or is it a compound?" Maja asked.

"No, it's like a village. Families live there, but we don't have a chief."

The men delivered the wagon to their employer in the centre of the town, and then they walked towards the outskirts on a much narrower road. It took them about thirty minutes to reach the location. It was just before sunset when they arrived, but the location was already darkened by a thick blanket of smoke from the evening fires. The houses were built so closely together that smoke from each home had no chance to rise in the individual plumes you could trace in a normal village. Here, it all coalesced and hovered in the air.

"There must be very many people living here," Polomane said as they entered the location and walked down the narrow lane towards the men's homes.

"No, not so many," one of the men replied.

Maja pulled Polomane's shirt from behind to caution him not to offend their hosts.

In the morning they joined the men and their families at church. Maja and Polomane positioned themselves strategically near the door so that they would be able to see each person who entered the building.

One by one, the congregation filed past – men first, followed by women in all sorts of headgear. Most of the young women wore brightly coloured headscarves, while the older ones wore white scarves or white Boer bonnets. Their dresses were long and wide, like Jenny Gonin's. Maja hadn't seen so many women in one place in a very long time. Suddenly he was scared. How would he recognise his sister?

Motumi had been just a flat-chested child when he last saw her. *Which one of these women can she be?* he wondered.

Although men and women entered through the same door, they soon separated and went to sit on opposite sides of the aisle that led to the pulpit in front. The women's side had built-in benches – long mounds that ran from the wall to the edge of the passage. There were no benches on the men's side. Each man brought in a small homemade bench and chose the most comfortable spot. It was best to sit against the wall so that they could lean against it when they released their big baritones during the singing of hymns or when they snoozed during the service. All the men wore jackets, but most were worse for wear or ill-fitting – definite cast-offs from their former masters.

The preacher came in by the side door, which led straight to the pulpit. Preacher July Bakkies was a short, stocky man with salt-and-pepper granules of hair dotted along the sides of an otherwise bald head. He was the senior *ouderling*, and he took himself very seriously, even though he was dressed in the same raggedy way as the other men. His point of distinction was a white tie that hung from his threadbare collar. How he got it, no one knew, because only qualified white dominees were entitled to the white tie. He didn't ascend the pulpit, as that was also the reserve of the visiting dominee. Instead, he stationed himself behind the collection table that stood in front of the pulpit.

The congregation stood up as preacher July took his position behind the table and a woman started a hymn. When they finished singing, the preacher stretched out his arms and bowed his head to pray.

"*Here God*," he intoned. "Open the hearts of these, Your folk, so that Your word can sink in. Give me the wisdom of Solomon to explain Your message. Amen.

"You may sit," he said authoritatively. Then preacher July picked up his Bible and turned towards the light from the door to read. There were only a few small windows in the walls, so the church was always a bit dark. Most people were not bothered about the lack of light because they could not read. Even preacher July's ability to read was the subject of many hushed arguments. Some people said that he'd learnt passages from the Bible off by heart and recited them, just pretending to read. It was true that the man's sermons were limited to a few texts, but this did not prove anything.

Stumbling and stuttering, he groped his way through the Word, which he chose from the Old Testament. Finally, he put the Bible down and started to explain the text. Free of the labour of reading, his speech took on a new verve.

"The children of Israel disobeyed God at their peril," he exploded, "and I think we are not too far behind ..."

For a full half-hour, preacher July expounded on the text – how the Israelites had brought damnation on themselves by worshipping idols instead of the living God. His voice ebbed and flowed like the ocean tide. A sweet smell of camphor slowly rose from the women's benches and hung in the air, casting a soporific effect over everyone. Like a seasick pendulum, a white bonnet in the front row started bobbing up and down, at first to the rhythm of the preacher's voice, then gradually to its very own slow beat.

"*God ... is ... God is liefde ... God is liefde,*" Maja muttered, as he tried hard to fight off the effects of the pungent fumes by practising his reading skills on the white letters embroidered on the red pulpit cloth.

Preacher July reached the climax of his sermon and leant forward on the table, his voice quivering as it climbed one decibel after another to emphasise the abominable disobedience of the community.

"I know what some of you are thinking!" he said, his eyes darting from left to right. "Yes, you are thinking: what has that got to do with us? But you! You!" he said, waving his stubby finger alternately at the men and women, "... have made yourselves modern gods.

"Beer!" he roared, glaring at the men. "Gossip!" he spat at the women. "Those are your gods! I know you men can't wait to go home and get drunk after church, and you women to go and spread dirty slander, but I must warn you, throughout the ages God has never failed to punish. Where do you think your sickness comes from ...?"

Suddenly he noticed the bobbing bonnet in the front row. He clung to the table and shouted firmly, interrupting his sermon, "Auntie Marta! Auntie Marta!"

Two young women sitting opposite Maja giggled and whispered, "That's it! Time to go home."

Auntie Marta's nodding always drove the preacher to his wit's end, so that he ended the service quickly.

Just after the final prayer, two men stood up, holding out collection bowls to the congregation. Coins were dropped in, and the men took them over to the preacher, whispering something in his ear. The preacher grimaced and asked the congregation to stand up for him to bless the offering, but before he started the blessing he lectured them on the poor collection.

"*Gemeente*, we must do better than this!" he warned. "The church cannot run on the measly pieces of copper you give!"

A woman started a slow hymn as the congregation began filing out. At this point Maja dashed up to the pulpit to ask the preacher to make a special announcement. The congregation stopped to watch the commotion. Maja whispered his request in the preacher's ear, and he responded immediately.

"Is there a woman here who came to this land as a young girl from the north?" he asked.

The women looked at each other, but no one came forward.

"I repeat: this man is looking for his sister. Is she here?" preacher July reiterated. "Please don't waste our time. We are hungry."

There was still no response from any of the women.

Maja then decided to take matters into his own hands, thinking that very few women would be willing to come forward to a total stranger. A thought suddenly came to his mind: *If nothing else will convince his sister of his identity, their clan praise poem should.*

He inched closer to the women's side and announced, "People, you don't know me, and you probably fear that I mean harm, but I don't. I'm *Maja a sekete sa boopelo, Mokone a ntshi dikgolo, Moloto molotolotsa batho bagabo a sa bare selo*! I intend no one any harm. My sister is all I'm looking for!"

A young woman in a red and blue headscarf moved out of her seat and approached the pulpit to stand next to Maja.

"Tshutshubu," she said softly, "is that you?"

"*My gonnas!*" Maja exclaimed. "Motumi!"

Only Maja's mother had used this term of endearment. Nobody had addressed him as Tshutshubu in over fifteen years. He reached over and hugged the young woman.

"Oh! Motumi *samma*, is this you?" Maja gasped. "*Allemagtig*, Motumi, I never thought I'd ever lay eyes on you again!"

Motumi hugged her brother and released an unstoppable spring of tears. The singer broke into another hymn – a more lively one this time. The congregation joined in, voices raised in thanksgiving for the reunion.

Maja and Motumi waited until the congregation had all left and she had pulled herself together.

"*Ouboetie*, I can't believe it! After all this time ... I used to think of you a lot when I first came here," Motumi gushed. "I thought of home and ... that night ... I wondered about you, always, and our parents, but it got too painful ..."

"I know, *sussie*, I know ..."

In a hurry to close the gap between herself and her brother,

Motumi chattered incessantly. "I don't know how the mind works," she said hurriedly, "but after a while it shut out all the painful things, and I only thought of things that were in front of me. Soon the new way of life, my new name, the food, the language, became part of me. I even learnt to be happy, and now, look, here we are together!"

Just then Polomane joined them, and Maja introduced the two: "Here's the reason for our journey," he said proudly, "my little sister Motumi."

"Come, come, Maja, don't use that name any more," his sister insisted. "I'm Christina now. This is what everybody here calls me. Please, call me Christina, sir."

"I'm very pleased to meet you, Christina," Polomane said, extending his hand to shake hers. "Your brother and I made an agreement a long time ago that we would find you."

Christina pulled her hand from Polomane's clutch, a little embarrassed about how long he'd held on to it. Noticing her discomfort, Polomane put her at ease by slapping Maja on the back and supporting her comment.

"My friend here insists that we change our names and go back to the old ones," he chuckled. "I used to be called September. Now it's Polomane, but I don't really care for all this change in names. If they can be changed so easily, like a dirty shirt, then they are not really important. They just sit on my skin …"

Christina nodded in agreement. "We can't turn back the clock by changing our names," she said. "My heart will always smile when I hear the name my mother gave me, but I'm not the same girl who left home."

"Listen, you two," Maja interrupted. "I don't want to talk too much about this, but some things have to be put right before we can go on with our lives. Names identify; names—"

"*Ag*, let's go before he starts," Christina said, as though the three were old friends. "I agree with you, Polomane, names don't change a person. Look at him, he's been through so many names, but he hasn't changed. He's always enjoyed listening to his own voice."

Polomane and Christina laughed as Maja started to make his way out of the church.

Christina led the way to her abode. As they walked, she sketched out the details of her life. She explained that she was living with a woman by the name of Auntie Maria, who had received her at the farm when she first arrived after the booking in Rustenburg. The woman and her husband Cornelius had been like parents to Christina. She'd lived an acceptable life on a single farm until two years previously, when her master sold up and went to live in Bloemfontein. Christina was sold to a neighbouring farmer and married off to a man old enough to be her father. The man died soon after.

"I don't know whether to say fortunately or unfortunately," Christina said, hinting that the marriage had not been harmonious.

"I then came to the location to live with Auntie Maria," she continued. "Now I work from her house. I pick up three white families' laundry and do it from home."

"Auntie Maria sounds like a good woman," Maja said.

"She is indeed," Christina replied. She went on to explain that all the people who lived in the location were *inboekselings* who used to live and work on Boer farms. At some point, they had been "relieved" of their duties – either because they were too old to be of further use, or because of some other arrangement. Since they had lost contact with their original villages, they settled in the nearest place where people like them lived.

"That's why their settlement is called a location and not a village," Christina said.

The threesome had lunch with Auntie Maria, who was so pleased to see Christina's brother that she served all the food for the festivities, forgetting to save some for her sons. They spent all afternoon chatting and drinking coffee under the peach tree. In the evening Auntie Maria insisted on having them stay over.

"There's enough room," she said. "You'll share the *voorhuis* with the boys."

The house had two rooms: the *voorhuis* or living room, which also doubled as a kitchen, and a bedroom, which she shared with Christina.

The men stacked the benches and everything that took up valuable sleeping space on the table so that they could sleep on the floor.

"I don't think we should test these people's hospitality too much," Polomane said to Maja the next morning. "It'll take a long time before we find jobs and our own places to stay."

"I agree," Maja replied. "We have to go back. I still have use of the cottage that Gonin offered me. Christina can help look after their child while we join the men at the camp, at least until we are better organised."

In the meantime, like most other missionaries, Gonin had decided to buy a farm. The missionaries felt that the best way to sidestep problems with the Boer government was to operate from private property. When Gonin met a man called Putter who was selling a farm not too far from Chief Kgamanyane's village of Moruleng, he immediately applied for permission from the Cape Synod. The Synod agreed, as they were also beginning to worry about the wisdom of keeping him idle in Rustenburg.

Putter's farm, called Welgeval or Welgevallen, was situated within the valley of the Pilanesberg mountain range and not too far away from a number of African villages, which Gonin felt was auspicious for the establishment of his mission station. He was also grateful that the farm was ensconced in the mountains, because it offered him peace, safety and a good deal of distance from all the Boer strife in the Transvaal. Gonin paid Putter 150 pounds sterling, and on the 10th of October 1864, ownership of Welgeval was officially transferred to him.

16

POLOMANE

I saw a trap opening, its jagged teeth bared, ready to bite and ensnare. I wasn't going to let that happen. I had risked my life, leaving that man Mostert lying on his back like a sack of mielies. I wasn't going to hand myself over to another Boer with my eyes wide open.

I will remember the hour I left Boshoek for the rest of my living days. I didn't plan it, but it had been fermenting in my mind for far too long – ever since Maja and I agreed on telling our masters that we wanted to leave. I spent every minute of God's days mentally rehearsing how I would tell baas Mostert the news, until it bubbled over on that fateful morning at the kraal. We were busy removing the blowfly larvae from the nose of a heavy heifer when I lost control of my tongue.

"Baas," I heard my mouth say, "I've been told that the law allows me to leave the farm now that I'm old enough."

He ignored me and continued digging the worm from the cow I was holding for him. Once I'd said it, I felt emboldened. I wasn't going to let him intimidate me.

"Baas," I repeated. "I want to go and start a new life for myself. The law says I can."

Without a word he turned around and released, across my face, the hottest *kafferklap* – a backhand slap reserved for black folk. I felt two drops of warm liquid trickle from my nose and reached up to wipe it. My hand was covered in blood. When I saw it, the rest of the liquid flowing inside me boiled and something inside my head exploded. I pushed the cow aside and lifted Mostert off his feet by his shirt, holding him aloft while my brain tried to calculate what to do with him.

"*Jou skelm*," he choked. "Put me down, *kaffer*."

I heard the fear in his voice and it spurred me on. I plonked him down and let loose the right hook I used for annoying calves that wanted to suck while I was milking. He sank to the ground like an innocent man, and I ran to my hut, picked up my few possessions and disappeared. He must have lain there until he came to. It doesn't seem as if anybody found him, as we were so far away from the house. Mostert was a proud man. He would never admit to anyone that I'd struck him. I suppose he told the community that the cow had attacked him. I know he was quietly looking for me, even though my friends have never sent word to that effect.

Now that wretched Maja, with all his schemes, wants us to work for another Boer, and soon Mostert will come and visit him on his farm. They always keep together, the Boers. What I don't understand is why I traipse after Maja. This morning I sat there quietly on the front stoep listening to him and this new Boer Gonin planning that we should work for him. That will be over my dead body, I promise you. The gall these Boers have; they see you and immediately want your hands. Maja may have seemed to be resisting, but I don't trust him. He's much too tame; he trusts too easily. Soon he'll give in to that Boer. I'll have to take him aside and talk to him very strongly.

I like Maja very much. He's more than a friend to me. I kept my strength over the past five years on Mostert's farm only because I always looked forward to the fun we had together when the masters were in church. He is funny, even a bit peculiar, and I enjoy his jokes. I think I've seen a new polite side of him now that his sister is accompanying us. I must say I also feel different in Christina's presence. I don't know what it is about women, but they make you feel clean – like you've just changed your shirt. I like that, maybe because I haven't had many of them around in my life. Our trip from Potchefstroom was so much more civil than when the two of us jackals travelled down on our own. I still think that, unless Maja does something completely unacceptable, I'll join them, but I'll have to watch that fast-talking joker. Somebody needs to.

Maja was firm about not joining Gonin on his farm, but the man's a smart Boer. He suggested that we let the women have the last word. He obviously knows we'll just go along with what they decide. Maja is still trying to create a good impression with his sister, so I'll have to be firm with him about the matter. I was glad Gonin went into the house to continue with his writing and left Maja and me sitting outside. At least I could have my say in private.

"Well, what do you think?" Maja asked, as soon as Gonin disappeared into the house. "Are you sure we are not rejecting an offer we'll regret?"

"Definitely. Why should we go back into slavery?"

"Come now, don't exaggerate. The man is offering us land to settle on. He's not trying to abduct us."

"I don't care what he says," I replied. "I've seen enough of them to know that they can never be trusted."

"But Gonin is different," Maja argued. "He joins in when he finds you working, he speaks to you like a human being, and he's the only white man who's ever insisted I call him meneer. I think he's a good man."

"Listen, Maja," I said firmly, "you are too tame for your own good. Maybe it's because you spent your life with one Boer. I don't care whether he wants to be called meneer or sweetheart, I'll always sleep with one eye open with him around."

"Maybe you're right, but—"

"No buts about it," I said. "These people are all the same."

"We could just give it a try," Maja tried. "We could just travel with them. We won't be obliged to stay."

"Maja, my friend, you can travel the length and breadth of the country with them and they will treat you reasonably, but all that falls away as soon as they reach the safety of their own farm."

"Well, that's settled then. We won't go," he conceded at last.

I was glad to put the matter to rest.

"But what if Christina wants to?" he chirped a minute later, refusing to let the matter die.

Then, as if the gods themselves had planned it, Christina came through the front door and joined us.

"That Mevrou Gonin is a very nice lady," she remarked, smiling broadly and taking a seat beside her brother.

"Hmph," we both grunted.

"I wouldn't mind going to work for them on their farm," she confessed. "After all, we are still going to have to find jobs and work for somebody. She said she'd like us to join them. What do you think?"

There it was: out. We had to think fast.

Maja handed the matter straight over to me. "I don't know," he said. "Ask Polomane."

"What do you think, *ouboet*?" she said, lifting her face up to mine.

"Weeell," I scratched my head, trying to find the right words. It wasn't as easy as it was with Maja.

"I think it's a good idea," she said, without waiting for my answer. "It's not like any old white couple that we don't know. Maja knows them well. I think we should go."

"I'm not sure about that, Christina," Maja said, hoping for support from me. "We have to give ourselves a chance to do things as we want. We have spent our lives being told what to do."

"Oh, let's try it out," she continued. "They said they'd give us a piece of land to build our own houses. I would really like that."

We were both silent, scuffing our feet in the dust and mulling over the idea. Christina adjusted the *doek* on her head and examined our faces for a reaction.

"Look at it this way, you two," she said. "We'll tell the Gonins that we'll just help them settle and that we want to come back to Rustenburg. Travelling with them will give us more time to get to know them and to decide if settling with them will be a good idea."

The woman certainly had a point. I suppose there couldn't be too much harm in such an expedition.

"That's fine," I agreed, looking at Maja. "I see your sister is smart."

"Excellent," Christina smiled. "I'll go and tell them that we're going."

"But, Polomane ..." Maja began, looking at me disbelievingly.

It was too late. The Gonins' front door closed after Christina's swishing skirt.

17

"*Hok ... hokaai!*" Van Staden shouted. A dozen oxen pulling a tented wagon stopped in front of the Gonins' house. Two *voorloper* boys turned and pushed the front oxen back to halt their movement. Van Staden, a local whom the Gonins had decided to employ as farm manager of Welgeval, hurried over to the front door and knocked loudly, annoyed at the fact that there was no one outside waiting for him.

The couple had overslept after a restless night with their baby. When Gonin heard the wagon arrive, he jumped out of bed and rushed outside to meet the man.

"Don't tell me you were still sleeping," Van Staden said. "We should be on our way by now."

Before Gonin could make his apologies, Maja and Polomane came out from the back room to help load the wagon.

"Who are these?" Van Staden enquired disdainfully. "We have enough help. Go!" he shouted, waving Maja and Polomane away from the wagon.

"Listen here, Meneer van Staden," Gonin said in surprisingly good Dutch. "I'll decide who goes and who doesn't, not you. You will be taking orders from me, not the other way round. Let's get that straight right from the beginning."

"*Ai*, don't be so touchy," Van Staden replied. "I just want to get you to your farm soon."

The ox-wagon was soon packed with all the Gonins' belongings. A space near the tent opening was cleared for the two women and

Land of My Ancestors

child to sit on, and pots and pans were hung under the wagon for easy access at camping sites.

Gonin and Van Staden rode ahead of the wagon to identify a safe route, free of boulders and dongas, while Polomane and Maja walked on the sides, driving the oxen.

Polomane cracked the long whip twice to get the span of beasts moving. The tent bumbled from side to side as the long line of animals lurched forward, pots and pans banging and clanging loudly against each other, and the young *voorlopers* straining to keep the trek on course.

The sun was still low on the eastern horizon. At a steady pace, they would reach Boshoek by evening, but Gonin did not want to travel that fast.

"I really don't think we need to be going very fast," he said to Van Staden. "We are going to this place to settle, so let's not move like people who will be coming back. I want us to enjoy our ride to the ... to the promised land, if I can say it like that."

"Whatever you want is fine by me," said Van Staden, who now thought better of contradicting his new employer.

They arrived in Phokeng by lunch time. The riders went ahead to seek a camping site along the banks of the little stream that ran through the village. Gonin rode up and down the river and looked at the sun to try to ascertain the time.

"It is still so early. Let us go on," he announced. "We'll stop for camp near the Kgetleng River."

"Your word is my command," Van Staden replied.

Polomane overheard the discussion about their route, which would take them through Boshoek in the middle of the afternoon. He decided there was no way he was going to travel through the village in broad daylight and risk bumping into Mostert. Local farmers usually invite trek parties for a meal or bring them food. So he decided to carve a separate and more discrete route for himself alongside the wagon.

He handed the whip to Maja and said, "We have absolutely nothing to eat for supper. Someone must think of taking charge here. I'll go and see what I can trap for us. You know I'm a better hunter than you."

With this excuse, Polomane disappeared into the bush, emerging now and again with a dead guineafowl or rabbit for the trekkers.

Just as the sun touched the hills in the west, they reached the banks of the Kgetleng, a crafty and erratic river. Without knowledge of where exactly to cross, people often fell victim to its unexpectedly deep pools. Villagers also believed that four-eyed snakes, which could pull you in if you dared to stare them in the eye, lived in these waters. The summer rains had been pelting down all of the previous week, and the river was almost bursting its banks, rushing down and crashing over rocks, making a great noise. The mystical mountains of Pilane stood lofty and dark blue against the evening sky.

This was Maja's and Polomane's territory. They knew better than to urge the party to cross the river, as Gonin was hoping, instead convincing them to camp on the southern side, so they could wait and study the river's plan. Gonin was disappointed that he'd still be breathing air from Rustenburg, but Van Staden consoled him by pointing out that he could at least see the mountains that embraced his farm.

Big fires were lit to keep away the beasts and mark off human territory. This was the land of leopard, lion and the small but equally fearsome hyena.

Young Augustus Gonin did not seem to enjoy the relocation. He had been restless, crying for most of the afternoon. Jenny had run out of ideas to comfort him, so Christina offered to put him on her back and rock him to sleep.

Polomane was resting under a tree, watching the two women exchanging the baby. Christina walked a small distance away, singing lullabies to the infant. Polomane sat up to get a better view of the scene. This was a sight that farm hands like him rarely beheld, and, watched at such leisure, it stirred unfamiliar feelings of hope in him. He closed his eyes and visualised himself working in the background and keeping watch on his family at the same time. It looked and felt very good.

They inspanned early the next morning and set off once more, travelling for some distance along the grassy banks, looking out for a shallow part through which to cross. The riders ahead spotted an inlet and signalled the *voorlopers* to steer the wagon towards it. They waded in, and in no time they were on the other side. Meneer Putter, the former owner of the farm, had promised to meet them at Matooster, a small trading site situated not too far from the river. They needed him to lead them through the gorges of the Pilanesberg mountains and show them the farm borders.

By mid-morning they had been waiting in Matooster for three hours already, and still Putter did not come. Gonin, no longer willing to camp on somebody else's land, decided that they should move on. For a while they skirted the edge of the Pilanesberg, seeking an entry point to its heart where the farm lay in wait. At last a gaunt valley, set between two high mountain slopes, appeared before them and they crawled through, with heavy cold air sliding down from the top. The riders squeezed the column of oxen from either side to keep them in line through the gorge, while the two *voorlopers* nosed around for a safe path. Van Staden ordered the women to get off so that the wagon was light enough for Maja and Polomane to heave it over the boulders that lay in the way.

They pressed forward, meandering around the twisted mountains,

Botlhale Tema

grimly determined to set final camp on Welgeval before it grew too dark. Finally, they emerged into a wide flat valley with a much lower set of hills in the distance. The riders sought shelter and a drinking place for their oxen.

All of a sudden, Gonin fell on his knees and kissed the ground, thanking God for keeping them safe through the darkness of the valley. Without a map to show them the borders of the farm, he relied on his sixth sense for their location, and it told him that this was it – his farm. The party had a quick supper and lay down to sleep, too tired to celebrate.

Maja woke up early the next morning and started the fire for coffee. They were all sitting around enjoying their first cup when a rider came galloping through the mountains.

It was Putter, visibly distressed that he had missed them the day before.

"Dominee Gonin, will you ever forgive me?" he pleaded. "I thought our appointment was for today. I'm really sorry, but I see you made it through that treacherous gorge intact."

"Oh, you must not worry, Mr Putter," Gonin replied, beaming. "I'm glad to welcome you on my farm, Welgeval."

"No, no, no, sorry Dominee, but Welgeval lies beyond those little hills over there." Putter gestured towards the hills behind Gonin.

"What!" Gonin exclaimed, turning around. "Where?"

"Yes, Meneer Gonin," Putter confirmed. "Welgeval lies inside the second ring of the Pilanesberge."

"Oh, no, I think we should go right away," Gonin replied. "I want to get there before midday."

"Yes, indeed, we'll get there before then."

The oxen were soon inspanned, the pots hung back under the wagon, and, assured by Putter's presence, the trekkers set off on their last lap. He led them to a narrow track that wound along a small stream. In no time at all, a circle of hills much lower than the Pilanesberg mountains shut off the wide valley on which they had been travelling, but the stream cut through the hills, creating a kind of highway. The party went through and entered a smaller valley nestling inside, completely encircled by these smaller hills.

"Here we are at last!" Putter announced. "On Welgeval!"

"Thank you, Lord, thank you!" Gonin shouted, punching the air. "I hope I'll serve You and never disappoint You in this, Your chosen place!"

He rode ahead to find a spot that would touch his heart. The stream cut the valley into two halves, an eastern and a western one. The western half was higher and rougher, with rocky outcrops and bare patches of granite spills interspersed between thickets of karee, wild olive, *Mongela* and *Mmilo* trees. Very tall elephant grass made its way among the leftover spaces. The eastern half was flatter and thickly blanketed with trees, making it more suitable for farming.

Gonin rode further northward on the western slope, and almost in the middle of the farm he came to a circle of tall wild olive trees just above the stream.

"This is it!" he shouted. "No further."

The trek party joined him, outspanning the oxen and offloading the goods under the olive grove. Gonin retrieved his Bible from his baggage and ordered everybody to stand for his first church service on Welgeval.

18

MAJA

How shall our grandchildren judge the value of Welgeval? Will it be by its produce, or simply by the exhilaration we experienced as we entered this hidden treasure? Perhaps I should just speak for myself. As we narrowed our way into Welgeval, I felt like I was walking back into my mother's womb, where all, I presume, is of the same kind of warm silence that met us. A stubborn peace hung over the place, punctuated only by the loerie bird's rudeness. "Go away! Go away!" it screamed, but it did not disturb the peace. I heard crickets chirping in the background – unusual, because normally they are sounds of the night. I bent down to smell the soil and perhaps sense its stories, but only the silence hummed.

"I think I'll stay," I said to myself, closing all options that I'd kept open up until that point.

Gonin opened his Bible and read a long text from Exodus – many verses about the children of Israel's journey from Egypt, the land of bondage. He compared our journey to theirs. He went on and on with this comparison, while all of us stood under the canopy of tall wild olive trees in an enclosure, which, from then on, was marked a holy spot. Finally, he asked us to kneel down and pray. This we did on one of the bare rocky patches, the rough surface of which Gonin seemed happily oblivious.

"Father," he began, "I want to thank You for this land, this piece of ground where I build Your church. The strength of rock here … may it be as prophetic for Thy works as Peter Your disciple's name was for …"

Gonin took off in a prayer that matched his chosen scripture. I'd thought Oubaas Venter said the longest prayers, but Gonin's beat everything I'd ever heard, and the sharp little pebbles on which we knelt stretched out each word, doubling the length of the prayer. Twice I opened my eyes and, as if on cue, Polomane did as well. We winked at each other to acknowledge our pain, but Gonin continued. Each conclusion of a sentence promised the end of the prayer, but for Gonin it was only a pause for breath before taking off on a higher note.

January, the young *voorloper* boy, started scratching himself rather noisily. Baby Gonin began to whimper, forcing his mother off her knees. Christina broke into a cough, and Polomane opened his eyes to observe the coughing seizure. At last, Gonin took note of the restlessness and pronounced the much-awaited word, "Amen".

Almost rolling off our knees, we sat down to orientate ourselves and check the wisdom of our final choice. A cool evening breeze whispered a silent message through the leaves of the trees. There were no forebears to advise us. We would have to decide through experience.

On the face of it, the site seemed ideal. The water was near enough: the small stream ran alongside the camp on the east, marking one border. The tall trees provided overall shelter and shade for the daytime. Short khaki bushes created an enclosing wall. Boulders and rocks stood guard on the hills, keeping away the beasts and bothers of the Transvaal. The soil on either side of the river also seemed free of the granite layer that covered most of Welgeval, making it suitable for gardening and larger-scale ploughing. Everyone was satisfied.

Van Staden immediately took up his role as farm manager. He

dispatched January and September, the young *voorlopers*, to collect slow-burning wood, so that we could make a fire that would last us through the night. Meneer Putter had warned us that Welgeval was partly owned by leopards. We sat around the fire, and the combination of fatigue and heat slowly mellowed us, so much so that our conversation began to scatter in different directions.

"I think the next winter will be severe. That moon ..." Polomane mused as he picked up the pot of boiling water and handed it to January and September to make coffee.

Christina unwrapped the bread and cut pieces for each of us.

"I hope that howling hyena stays where he is," she said, her eyes peering into the dark. "Do we have enough wood?"

"We'll have to build quickly so that the first rains don't catch us ..."

"I think the baby is asleep now ..."

Jenny placed the sleeping baby next to her. A thick darkness descended on us before we had even finished our meal. We laid out our mats and slept, I think, so soundly that we made up for all the years of sleep lost on the Boer farms.

Gonin must have done all his planning in his sleep, because the next morning he greeted us with some firm decisions.

"I would like to build my house just above those willow trees there ..." he said, pointing into the valley, "... not too far from the stream. I will build the church here where we are now standing."

"*Goed*, Dominee, I'll get the boys to start digging the foundation right away," Van Staden responded. "On second thought, I'll split them up. That tall one ... what's his name? Polo ... will have to go and dig the trees and lay out the vegetable garden or else we are going to starve."

"Yes, your idea of the garden is good," Gonin replied. "You go and work with the boys. I want Maja to come with me to the villages today, so we can find out about the chiefs."

And so began our first day on Welgeval.

19

The trekkers settled into a daily routine of rolling rocks, digging and building. In two weeks, Gonin's four-roomed house, complete with a small stoep, had been erected. The two young *voorlopers* were given a new assignment: to cut some of the elephant grass for thatching. The grass, a thick hissing blanket in the breeze, covered every inch of Welgeval.

While all of this activity was going on, Gonin decided to pursue his true reason for buying the farm, not wanting all the building and settling to undermine his main aims. He immediately started setting off on regular trips to the surrounding villages of Magong and Ramatshabalemao to introduce himself to the chiefs. A month later he got in touch with his superiors to register his presence on the farm and, with Maja's help, penned a brief record of the progress he'd made.

Welgeval
12 September 1864

My dear Brother in Christ,

I'm exactly a month on this wonderful Welgeval. I think we have no reason at all to regret having bought the farm where I believe I'll be able to work quietly and unmolested. I realise that I will have to act, especially in the beginning, with the utmost prudence, with a special assistance of the Lord, but I'm hopeful now that our work is fairly begun. I will not say that we shall not yet encounter difficulties and molestations, but the Lord will provide. And even though this commencement is very, very small not to say insignificant, oh, that by the blessing of the Lord it may be found like the mustard seed becoming a great tree.

Hoping and trusting that your support will flow to me forever.
Yours in Christ,
Henri Gonin.

Gonin's goals were finally in view, but his manager, Van Staden, couldn't adjust to life with only the Gonins and the five "natives". He left Welgeval suddenly, barely giving a week's notice. But everything continued according to plan. A light shower of fertility seeped through Welgeval's soil, and Gonin was blessed with the arrival of a daughter.

The question of whether Maja, Polomane and Christina would stay on Welgeval for good, or just long enough to help Gonin settle, remained hanging in the air. None of the three had come out clearly on the issue. They all went on with their daily duties as if the question did not exist, and the urgency to decide, which they had felt so acutely when they first arrived, seemed to fade into the hills.

Maja noticed this silent consensus, but decided not to take anything for granted. He would demand a definite answer from each of them. After two months on Welgeval, he confronted the two.

"So, when do we go back to Rustenburg?" he asked, one evening as they sat around the fire. "Gonin is settled enough now. We can make our way back to Rustenburg as we agreed at the beginning."

"Don't be ridiculous, Maja," Polomane replied. "How can we leave now that Van Staden has gone?"

"True," Christina agreed. "That would be cruel. How do you think these people will manage alone on this farm?"

"Are you saying you are going to settle on Welgeval?" he asked, getting straight to the point. "No more Rustenburg? Are you comfortable with the man now, Polomane?"

Maja turned to face his friend, but Polomane remained silent. He'd become so accustomed to the day-to-day rituals of the farm that this was the first time he'd properly confronted the issue.

"What do you want us to say, Maja?" Christina interrupted with some irritation.

"Just asking, *sus*," Maja replied calmly. "I'm sure Gonin is anxious to know as well."

"Obviously we'll stay," Polomane announced. "Just tell him that, and when you do, you might ask about the land he promised to give us."

"Well, I'm glad to know," Maja replied, standing up and looking towards the last remnants of sunset. "We can't go on from day to day without making plans. I think Gonin will be happy to hear about our decision too. Just between us, I would like to settle on the western side, not too far from Gonin's house, because I have to help him with his work. I think I'll build my house just off the main camp, but further west. What do you think?"

"Ja, ja, that makes sense," Polomane agreed. "You always have to go off early with him on his trips, so it's best to be near him."

"What about you? Which side do you prefer, Polomane? We must tell Gonin our preferences."

"It's really up to the man," Polomane answered, "but I hope to spend my time working in the fields and tending the cattle when we finally have them. I don't want to be too far from my work."

"But where exactly?" Maja pressed.

"You see much of the land on the east of the river has already been cleared for the mielie fields," Polomane explained, pointing towards the desired location. "That's where I should build my house."

"And what about me?" Christina chirped.

"*Sus*, you know I promised never to let you out of my sight again," Maja replied. "So what are you worrying about?"

Christina continued to stay with the Gonins, while her brother and Polomane built their own houses. Maja and Gonin were often away in the villages, inviting locals to attend the school and church. Polomane and the two young boys did most of the farm work. They dug furrows to lead water from the stream to the Gonins' vegetable garden. Because they started very early on different parts of the farm, they agreed to have lunch together every day to discuss their progress and make new plans. However, because of visits to the villages, Polomane was often the only one who had lunch with Jenny and Christina.

On these occasions, Christina would be hanging out baby Augustus's napkins to dry when Polomane arrived for lunch. He would sit quietly on a bench next to the house and watch her work. She was a smaller but much more refined version of her brother – dark-complexioned, with a more chiselled nose. She wore her hair in thick braids. Although most of her hair was covered by a white headscarf, which she'd made from a cut-open mielie bag bleached in the sun, sometimes a few braids escaped. Except for her arms, the rest of her body was hidden under a long black dress.

Often, without even turning around, Christina sensed the man's presence and would begin to chatter and comment on this or that aspect of their new life as soon as he arrived. He noticed how she often became excited about things that many people didn't care about. One day when he arrived she took him by the hand to show him a perfectly round bird's nest, which she had discovered in one of the willow trees. Two weaver birds were perched right next to it.

"Do you see those two little birds over there?" she enquired. "Are they honey guides?"

"No, they are weaver birds," Polomane replied. "That nest belongs to them."

"Look at them, they seem to be talking to each other," she continued animatedly. "Do you think they can understand each other? I could swear they can. What do you think?"

"It's a language I don't understand, if ever they do talk," Polomane answered dryly.

"Just look at them, *ouboet*, twittering like that, they really sound like they are sharing a secret," Christina enthused. "Do you think they are both females?"

She turned to look at him and, before he could respond, concluded, "I think they are."

"How on earth would I tell between a male and female bird?" Polomane replied, completely astounded by Christina's interests. "Christina, *vroumens*, why do you care what birds say to each other?"

"What did you say? Do you agree they are both females?" she responded, insisting on an answer.

"Yes, they are," Polomane said to appease her, but how in heaven's name was he supposed to tell if a bird is a male or female, he wondered. He left her standing under the tree and went back to sit on the bench.

What's this about Christina, she is so quiet among people, but put her outside and then she's all attentive and excited about animals and birds, Polomane continued to ponder as he gazed at her.

Watching Christina doing her chores at lunch time slowly became a more important reason for Polomane to interrupt his day's work than the meal itself. He started observing her movements much more closely as she went about her everyday tasks: bending, stretching, wiping her face, and so on.

Such thin arms and fingers, you wouldn't think she used them to wash that load. Women do it all so differently, he thought, *or is it just Christina?*

Polomane decided to watch Jenny as well, just to see if they did things in the same way. As soon as he'd made the decision, he changed his mind. Watching another man's wife like that would be rude.

He decided to take his lunch break a little earlier to give himself time to sit in the bushes and watch Christina longer. Sometimes, only sometimes, she would turn around with a smile on her face, as if to acknowledge a presence. The first time it happened, Polomane ducked and hid under the bush. He was so worried that Christina had seen him watching her that he didn't go to lunch at all that afternoon. But when it happened again, he decided to confront her and defend himself.

"I nearly fell in a warthog's hole back there where you saw me," he said, trying to ward off an accusation.

"Where?" she replied. "I never saw you."

"You did," he insisted. "I saw you smile when I stumbled."

"*Ouboet*," Christina said sternly, "if I say I didn't, then that's the truth."

"Oh, sorry, I thought you did," Polomane muttered, feeling his cheeks burn.

Polomane watched his feelings change, shifting daily from warm admiration to something so strong that it kept him awake at night. He wrestled with them, not sure what to do, but he was absolutely certain that he wouldn't risk displeasing Christina by telling her. Finally he decided to confide in her brother. He knew that Maja would make mischief with this new information, teasing and carrying on, but he concluded that it was still a much safer route.

Polomane tossed and turned more than ever on the night before he approached Maja. His courage staggered and faltered as he began to fear that he might jeopardise his friendship not only with Christina, but with her brother as well.

Go and look for a wife somewhere else, where you won't cause offence, he taunted himself.

But by morning, his resolve rose again with the sun. He would tell Maja about his feelings for his sister, and damn the consequences.

He started work very early, and planned his strategy as he dug and turned the soil. Like a trained dog, his body registered fatigue at exactly the right time to break for lunch. For a change, Maja had not accompanied Gonin on a trip to Rustenburg. He had been working in his garden, but was now resting under a tree inspecting the calluses on his hands. Polomane sat down next to him, determined to start the heart-to-heart. He took off his hat and placed it on his knees, and pulled out a blade of grass and quietly started chewing on it. Maja sensed an atmosphere being created and decided not to interfere.

After three minutes of silence, Polomane cleared his throat and looked at his friend with much seriousness.

"Maja," he began, "we've been friends for a long time, but what I have to tell you may undo all that. I beg you, hear me out."

He stopped to check Maja's reaction, but there was none.

"If you don't like what I have to say, just say so," Polomane went on. "I will accept it in the best of spirits."

"Just get on with it and stop all this *gekerm*," Maja replied.

"Maja, I think your sister is a wonderful woman and I'd really like to marry her," Polomane blurted out. "What do you think?"

"Hmm, you want to marry my sister?" Maja said indifferently.

The announcement did not surprise him too much. Polomane had been a changed man since Christina had joined them. Not only was he more clumsy, but he spoke even less frequently than before, and Maja often caught him gazing at his sister in a strange sort of trance.

Maja pulled his hat over his eyes and slid down a bit so that he was half-sitting and half-lying down. Sweat had eaten out holes around the crown of Maja's hat. He took advantage of one of them and squeezed a look at Polomane, enjoying seeing him squirm like a mopane worm in a hot pan.

"Please, Maja, it's just a thought," Polomane pleaded, praying that his feelings would not backfire. "And, like I said, it may be a very bad one."

Maja folded his arms on his chest and ignored the plea.

"Well, I've said it," Polomane said defiantly, annoyed by Maja's coolness. "Now you know what I feel about your sister. Just say whether you'll allow me to marry her or not."

"Hmm," Maja sighed, turning the screws a little tighter. He knew what this conversation was costing Polomane, but he also felt strongly that a wife shouldn't be handed over like a present. A man had to earn her.

For a brief few moments, everything was quiet on Welgeval – as if the land itself was also holding its breath in anticipation of an answer. A small honey guide darted past, whistling a tune so sharp it almost sounded like a warning, but then the usual duet of the loerie bird and the turtle dove broke the silence. Polomane held down an inner panic, his heart pounding and rattling in his ribcage. He swallowed and accepted his fate. He would lose his friends, and then lose himself to the world.

Just when he was about to stand up and leave, Maja sat up.

"My friend Polomane, previously known as September," he began. "You know that where I come from, marriage is not for snot-nosed boys who can't even fasten their own loin cloths. A man has to earn his wife, and I'd like to know what makes you think that you deserve to marry my sister?"

"Are you calling me a *snotneus*?" Polomane asked angrily.

"I never said that," Maja replied. "All I'm trying to tell you is that my sister deserves to be married to a man of some worth, and I'd like you to prove yours."

"If you don't know my worth by now," Polomane announced, rising to leave, "then forget it, it's too late."

Maja jumped up and waved a finger at Polomane. "You haven't even thought about it," he chided. "I know. You are just driven by what you feel for Christina. Now let me tell you, I have a very big condition for you to meet before you can marry my sister."

Irritated by the drama but intrigued about the condition, Polomane decided to hold his tongue and wait for Maja to finish talking.

"My condition or nothing! You make your choice!" Maja repeated emphatically.

"I'm getting tired of your weaving tongue," Polomane said. "Just tell me your *donnerse* condition before I do something I'll regret."

"Back home a man pays *bogadi* for a wife," Maja announced. "But what can you give me? You have nothing but the dust under your feet."

Polomane looked down at his dust-covered feet. There was some truth in his friend's words, but they stung nevertheless.

"I'm far from home and Christina is my only blood relative in this part of the world," Maja went on. "I don't even know if I'll ever get married, so whatever happens I'd like to strengthen my side of the family. My proposition is this: instead of paying *bogadi*, you should agree that we all become Christians, as Gonin wants. This will mean taking on Christian names, as well as what they call surnames, which are clan names really. Now this is where the condition comes: I want you to give up your clan name, Malema, and take on mine, Moloto, so that your children will go by that surname."

Maja glanced at Polomane to gauge his reaction, but the man's expression betrayed nothing. He had decided not to reply, hoping to give Maja a chance to tangle himself in his words.

"Now take it or leave it," Maja said dramatically, rounding off his speech by sloping down against the tree again. The farm hummed. Polomane was quiet.

Then Maja, who could never hold his tongue for very long, sat up again.

"This may sound harsh," he continued, "but think of it this way: this agreement will strengthen the bond between us even further. So what do you say?"

Polomane thought back to when he first met Christina in Potchefstroom and the discussion they had had about names. He remembered that they both agreed that names were nothing but coats that could be shed without making a difference to the person wearing them. Surely one shouldn't sacrifice a loving future just for a name?

"Listen Maja," he replied. "You have an odd passion for names, and I told you a long time ago that I don't care one way or the other. All I want is to marry your sister, and if by all this ..." he waved his arms around animatedly, "... this ... carry-on you meant that I can, then you can call me any name you want!"

"Yes, I meant that you can marry Christina," Maja confirmed. Then, not wanting to have his authority undermined, he added, "but what about becoming a Christian?"

"That I'll do for Christina because she is already one, and not for you," Polomane said. "In any event, Gonin won't allow us to stay on his farm if we don't."

"Now don't worry about the details," Maja replied, satisfied that his plan would be adopted. "As long as we agree on the important things."

The blue sky bent down to kiss Welgeval's brow, and the

mountains of Pilane glowed in a borrowed blue as they tasted first love permitted. The little honey guide chirped and squeaked with delight, while the loerie bird and the turtle dove erupted into an unbridled chorus of congratulations. For a moment Polomane lost his reserve and hugged Maja excitedly.

But he sobered up abruptly.

Christina has still not agreed, he remembered.

"How will I tell her?" he said worriedly.

"Don't you worry," Maja replied assuredly. "I can handle my sister."

"Oh, no, you won't," Polomane said firmly, fearing his friend's reckless enthusiasm. "I'll find a way to tell her."

"Go ahead," Maja scoffed. "But don't come whining to me after you've messed it all up."

"Good, I'd like us to prepare for this moment, be baptised and do all the things that will please her before I ask her."

And so the deal was done.

20

POLOMANE

I'd underestimated the whole business of baptism, and the *voorloper* boys had beaten us to it. They were already enrolled in Gonin's catechism classes together with some of the boys from the villages. Maja and I were excluded – and although this was mainly because Gonin wanted separate classes for youngsters and adults, it presented a serious obstacle.

To make matters worse, Maja was ready to be baptised ten times over, while I lagged behind. Whenever Gonin or Jenny couldn't take classes, he took their place eagerly and helped the students practise their writing skills. With all his involvement, his reading and writing, as well as his knowledge of the Bible, improved tenfold. I, on the other hand, who desperately needed this baptism, could barely read.

I was determined to marry Christina soon. I swore, *al bars die bottel*, nothing would stop me from getting that man Gonin to register me with his first baptism group. I decided to enlist Maja's help, even though I hated the thought of his usual posturing.

I rushed off to lunch much earlier than usual and was lucky to catch Maja just as he was inspanning the cart for Gonin and him to go to the village. They were on their way to confirm the list of boys for the baptism. Thank God ... just in time.

"Something I want to ask you, Maja," I said breathlessly. "Have you chosen your Christian name?"

"There's nothing to choose," he replied with his usual haughtiness. "I've decided and I've already told Gonin."

"What?" I pressed on.

"I've chosen Stephanus, after oubaas Stephanus Venter," he declared proudly. "That man saved my life and I'd like to honour his memory."

"I see," I said, and chose my next words carefully. "And what about me? You know we all agreed to become Christians."

"What about you indeed," Maja replied mockingly. "There's no hurry. You'll join next year's group."

Blood rushed to my head and pounded on my temples as I choked the intense desire to murder him. No one should want something like I wanted Christina to be my wife. It is quite dangerous. Maja noticed my struggle with my feelings. *Die slang*, how he enjoys torturing me like this. Suddenly he reverted to the kindness that brought us together and said: "Don't worry, *ou maat*, I'll talk to Gonin for you. I'm sure he'll agree to bring you in."

Just as I was about to grab his arm to thank him, he asked: "But what about your Christian name? Have you decided on one?"

My gonnas, I thought, *will I ever escape Maja's attachment to names?* But then I remembered that this time it was a requirement if I wanted to be a Christian. I had to think fast.

I'd hardly put two ideas together when Maja blurted out: "David! I think this name will suit you."

Of course, Maja wouldn't let an opportunity to control matters pass him by. But I liked the name. In fact, it was one of the few I'd toyed with after I learnt that I was up for another name change.

"I think I'll settle for David," I told him. "David and I have much in common: we are both strong and brave."

But, as before, I didn't care one bit for all the fuss. The new name and the baptism were just steps towards my happiness.

Land of My Ancestors

"I agree," he declared, as though it was a matter of grave importance. "David suits you. I'll tell Gonin about our decision."

"Hold up," I said, stopping him from climbing on the cart. "I'd like to be there when you tell him." I wanted to make sure that I wouldn't be misrepresented. This was too important a matter to leave to Maja.

"Good," Maja said, "let's go and introduce Gonin to David and Stephanus Moloto."

Gonin seemed surprised by our request, but mainly by my desire to be included in the baptism. He felt that I would need a much longer time to go through the catechism class. He rattled on and on about how much I had to learn, citing all the biblical verses I would need to know.

Now I was worried. I squashed my hat into a little ball and prayed. This man could not do this to me. I quickly interrupted his rambling to assure him of my abilities.

"Meneer Gonin," I said earnestly, "I haven't read anything in a long time, but I have learnt before. I'm sure I'll pick it up quickly as soon as we start again. Maja can also help in his spare time. I really don't want to be the only heathen on Welgeval."

"It's not about being left out, Polomane," he replied, shaking his head. "The heart must be ready."

"It's ready enough, Meneer," I responded, clutching my hat to my chest. "I came here at the same time as Maja, and I have listened to you preach every day. Except for the fact that I haven't been baptised yet, I am Christian at heart."

"Well, let's start first with the classes," Gonin conceded. "But I'm not prepared to have the baptism wait for a long time. I'd like to have more young people."

We then confessed our intention to share a surname, as well as my desire to marry Christina.

"Ah, so that is why you are hurrying!" Gonin exclaimed. "Well, I can see no problem with the surname or becoming brothers ... you are already like brothers. But the whole relationship will be difficult to explain when you marry Christina, Polomane."

Gonin started to shake his head again, and I thought for a moment he would change his mind about the classes.

"I can see that," I explained, "but I have to fulfil this condition before Maja will allow me to take his sister."

"I don't think it is too much of a matter," Gonin continued. "I'd rather have you baptised soon before you take this important step. You'll find a way around the relations matter."

He then expounded on the virtues of wedlock and the need to make Christ the foundation of marriage, patting me on the back as we walked to the door.

Everything was on track and I felt confident, but the person around whom everything revolved was not yet in the picture, let alone in agreement with my plans. I had to tell Christina. But when? I decided to wait until the day of my baptism, when, I presumed, all my luck would be with me.

For the next four weeks, I pored over the verses of the Bible, enduring hours and hours of Maja's extra instruction. My friend was only too delighted to show up all my shortcomings with his vast knowledge, calling me *agteros* and chuckling at my mistakes, but I just gritted my teeth and kept my eye on the final goal. On several occasions, I thought Gonin was going to hold me back, but my endurance paid off in the end. He let me through.

On Christmas Eve the four of us presented ourselves for baptism. We stood in front of Gonin in clean shirts, ready to wear our new names and, I hoped, for me to take the first step towards my new life.

As we went through the christening ritual, I was aware that Christina was watching, and, because she took church and religion so seriously, I was certain that she was proud of us. This boosted my confidence, and I decided to take her aside and reveal my heart to her as soon as the service was over.

But my plan to talk to her alone was scuppered. My new brother stuck with us all of that Sunday afternoon, gibbering on about the baptism and trying out our new names. I decided to hold out until the following day, when Maja would be away with the Gonins in Rustenburg.

When I arrived for lunch that afternoon, Christina was sitting alone on my usual bench. She had finished her work early because the Gonins had taken their children with them. I gazed at her for several minutes, imagining how the next hour could change my life. Maybe it was better to live in a distant dream of promise than to face rejection head-on. But I couldn't go on in silent agony. It was now or never.

I sat down under the tree opposite her.

I wasn't quite sure how I would start the conversation, but I'd learnt that the indirect way is always best, so I enquired about her health and went on to comment about the heat of the December month. All the time I was gauging her mood, but I couldn't quite read it. She answered my questions well enough, but she didn't pick up the conversation. I think she was surprised, because I was never the one to start all the talking. I decided to step back a little, keep quiet and make things appear as normal.

After a minute of silence, she asked, "Are you not well, *ouboet*?"

Daarsy, there was my opening.

"Yes, I'm all right, Christina," I began, "but sometimes I feel that Welgeval is a very lonely place. Are you sure you wouldn't want to go back to Potchefstroom?"

Christina inclined her head, obviously surprised by this thought. "Definitely not," she asserted. "Why do you think that?"

"Well, look at you sitting alone here," I said. "You are always on your own. Surely this is not a life for a nice young woman like you?"

"Now don't exaggerate," she said, frowning into the sunlight. "There are other people here, like my brother, yourself and the Gonins. I'm fine, even though I sometimes miss Auntie Maria. But I really like it here. It's so far from the life of uncertainty that I was used to. It's safe."

"Mmm," I sighed, "I also feel safe here."

I felt a small panic rise inside me. Our conversation had been going in the desired direction, but suddenly it seemed to peter out and disappear into this cloud of safety. I cleared my throat and grabbed it by the tail.

"Christina," I announced, "I don't want to offend you, but I'd like to know what you feel about the idea of a home with a companion and the possibility of a family."

"What's that?" she replied, as if she'd been sleeping.

"You heard me, Christina," I said.

"*Ouboet*, you're full of questions today," she smiled. "Where would I find a companion like that on Welgeval?"

This stumped me a bit. I did not expect to face such a question so soon. To give myself a chance to put the right words together, I took a little detour and asked about the Gonins.

"When will Gonin be back?" I enquired.

"They didn't say," Christina yawned. "The usual time, I suppose."

And then it occurred to me that she was just playing dumb. She understood my question perfectly. She wanted me to say it directly. Well, if that's what she wants, I decided, I'll hit it on the head.

I stood up and sat down next to her on the bench.

"Christina," I said again. "I've decided to settle down here on

Welgeval and I'd like you to be my wife. Will you marry me? Your brother has already given me his blessing."

"What!" she exclaimed. "You've been discussing me with my brother?"

I shifted a little closer to her on the bench, not about to be intimidated, and looked her squarely in the eyes.

"Christina," I said a third time, ignoring her question. "It would really make me happy if you agreed. I promise to look after you for rest of my life."

As our eyes met, I realised just how much I loved the woman. Until that moment I'd never fully appreciated her beauty. I'd always liked her eyes, like two moons on her face. Her sweet smile had always warmed my heart, but all of her taken together like this was simply wonderful, maybe because of my desperate hope that she would agree to be my wife.

She dropped her gaze and started drawing figures in the sand with her toes. Just when I was about to insist on an answer, she said, "I will be happy to marry you."

I took her hand and kissed it as I tried to explain the agreement I had made with her brother, but she was not interested. Christina did not see what difference a surname would make.

"I wish Maja would leave things alone," she said, as she pulled her hand away and stood up to go and dish up my lunch.

21

Gonin and Maja decided to put more energy into the mission work, while Polomane spent his time preparing ground for ploughing and adding a room to his original abode. Welgeval grew by three more families: the Motaungs, Malaus and Mokwenas. All of them had lived on Boer farms and came to the farm to seek asylum after their release. They were allotted land on the slopes of the hills in the north. After their baptism, the two *voorloper* boys, January and September, had also formed a family of sorts. Gonin had selected the names Petrus and Abraham for them, and they decided to adopt their village totem animal, Phiri, as a surname. As they were still responsible for jobs around Gonin's home, they built their houses close to his.

In June 1865, Reverend Charles Murray, the inspector of missions from the Cape, came to visit Welgeval and check on Gonin's progress in setting up the mission station. Gonin was proud to show him how he had tamed the wild. He had a few converts to present as well. Murray observed these "successes" with a critical eye and, in spite of Gonin's enthusiasm, was not impressed.

Too much focus on home life instead of the heavenly battle, he noted. He produced a harsh report as soon as he arrived back in the Cape, and dispatched it to Gonin immediately.

Gonin was on his weekly jaunt to Rustenburg, buying groceries and checking his mail, when he found a pile of letters waiting for him. He had many errands to make that day, so instead of using his lunch break to open the mail, he decided to do them all and ride back home early. He would have all the time to go through his correspondence while waiting for supper.

He arrived on Welgeval just after sunset and busied himself with the mail, while also entertaining his children. He was feeling particularly grateful that evening, because Welgeval had given him not only peace of mind, but also a healthy family since his arrival on the farm.

He saw the envelope from the Cape Synod and tore it open, excited to receive feedback from Murray.

"What!" he shouted, after scanning the letter. "This cannot be. It really can't. This is not right. What arrogance!"

"What is it, Henri?" Jenny asked, picking up the crying baby from the floor. "What is it saying?"

Gonin went over the terse little paragraph from Murray in which he questioned his capability as a missionary. It tore a strip off his heart, but instead of pain, it filled him with fury.

"Murray knows what it has cost us to get to this place," Gonin spat, handing the letter to his wife. "He saw ... in Rustenburg ... what we go through. Not enough! He did not see enough or he would know how we have suffered. He would know to be grateful. What is it that happens to a man when he becomes too high in his position?"

"What a man," Jenny sighed, as she read the letter. "I don't think he should make us worry too much, Henri. This is not reason."

"He did not abandon the cross because of all the insults ..." Henri quoted from the Bible to remind himself and his wife of the divine requirement of fortitude. The couple prayed fervently, and went to bed.

Gonin had come to appreciate the therapeutic value of their vegetable garden. Very early the next morning he joined Maja, who was already leading water from the stream. He picked up the hoe and thrust it repeatedly into the dry soil. Maja noticed the unusual energy expended on the task.

Something is amiss, he thought.

At last Gonin came up for breath. He leant against the handle of the hoe and looked fiercely at Maja.

"You remember when we have left Rustenburg," he said, wiping his brow, "there was talk that Kgamanyane is now keen to have me work in his village. I think we need to make our mission grow more. I would make more converts if I was working in a bigger village ... like Saulspoort. Do you think so also?"

"Hmm, I hear what you say," Maja answered, quite amazed by this unexpected conversation.

What brought this on? he wondered.

"I really think this would be good," Gonin went on. "Even the Cape Synod is saying so."

"Ah, the Cape Synod," Maja said, appreciating the logic. "Well, we could ride to Moruleng to find out ... nothing stopping us."

"Right," Gonin said, throwing down the hoe. "First I write a letter to Murray so I can post it when we are riding. Tomorrow morning, as soon as we are awake, we must go to Moruleng."

Gonin marched away from his beloved garden and sat down inside, where he poured out his feelings to Murray:

Welgeval
July 1865

Dear brother in Christ

Your letter reached me today and I cannot believe your failure to appreciate the challenges I faced to reach this point in my work. Place yourself in my situation. Newly arrived from Europe, after having left all those who are dear to me, still a novice in the work of the ministry, alone in a country where I found so to say no friend, no sympathy, no encouragements, not knowing the language of the land, left almost entirely to myself, having almost no directions from the Committee, restrained by the intolerant laws of the country, without a fixed field of labour, in the midst of a time of civil war, looked upon with suspicion by all parties, slandered by many – who would not in such a position have felt as I did, sometimes discouraged and distressed? Who would not sometimes have been dismayed by the feeling that one is entertained by a church without being able, with the best will, to do much? May the D. R. Church of the Colony remember that a Church who gives for the propagation of the Gospel, its prayers, its money, its men, does not get any poorer.

Oh that the church would nurture its workers a little more like Christ expects.

Yours truly,
Henri Gonin.

The following morning, the pair set off from Welgeval just as the sun was rising. They rode hard, eating up the distance, with the hope of finding the *kgotla* still in session.

Chief Kgamanyane and his men had a difficult case of stock theft to settle. They had deliberated over it for two days now, but every time a decision seemed near, one of the men would scupper it with a new question for consideration. The chief's youngest wife and her aides ferried endless pots of beer to the *kgotla*, and the men, who always brought their skins to work on during meetings, were now sitting with soft pieces of leather on their laps. The chief was also growing quite impatient.

"Bakgatla," he said irritatedly, "we've chewed through this

matter to the marrow. We need to come to a conclusion. If we are unable take a collective decision, then I will do it myself. The case is simple: there is ample evidence that Ramorogo stole the cattle. Those who question this truth must produce evidence to the contrary."

The chief was just about to make a ruling when a messenger appeared, announcing Gonin's and Maja's arrival.

"Did you say Gonin is here? What can I say? Think of a rhino and look out for a tree!" the chief exclaimed, waving his fly whisk.

He had been meaning to bring this matter of theft to an end so that he could discuss the introduction of "the book" with his villagers.

"Now our gods have sent the man I've been thinking about," he remarked. "Please let them enter."

Gonin and Maja came in and introduced themselves to the *kgotla*. Maja began to outline the purpose of their visit, but before he was given a chance to expound on the virtues of Gonin's offer, the chief interrupted and told him to keep it short.

"I have discussed this matter of the book with Chief Mokgatle of Bafokeng," he explained. "We have already agreed that it would be good for our children to learn to talk to the book. They will need it to get to the heart of the white man's secret."

Gonin then tried to launch into an explanation of the Bible's virtues, but Chief Kgamanyane again cut him short.

"With all the problems I've had with this man Kruger, I wouldn't mind learning myself," he declared. "So, Gonin, I think you should go home, collect your goods and come and work here in the main village of the Bakgatla."

Gonin and Maja thanked the chief and the *kgotla* for their time. They set off for Boshoek to post the letter to Murray, and then returned to Welgeval. Gonin was quiet for most of the way, and Maja did not wish to disturb his thoughts. The Cape Synod's wishes had been adhered to, but lives at Welgeval would be thrown out of kilter. Major adjustments had to be made. Silently they rode westwards, eyes squinting against the setting sun.

22

The birth of their son took them by surprise. Christina had spent the day buzzing around as usual, showing no signs of anything imminent. The first indication of trouble came far into the process, when it was almost too late to call for help. Polomane had to jump out of bed to go and fetch the local midwife, Kaatjie Mokwena, in the middle of the night.

"How could the child come normally when his mother never sat still?" Kaatjie said, blaming this sudden turn of events on Christina's hard work.

Polomane and Christina had not known a moment's rest since they were married. It seemed they could not wait to have all the things they'd always dreamt about. They worked all day on Gonin's fields, and then did their own chores in the evening. Polomane added a second room to the original hut and was considering a stoep for hot summer afternoons. Two chairs were standing half-finished under the tree.

Christina dug a vegetable patch next to the house and every evening she laboured over her produce, fetching water from the stream to water her pumpkin and bean seedlings. It was not really surprising that all the energy bubbled through to the child, with the result that he popped out unexpectedly early.

"And what shall he be called?" Kaatjie asked, as she handed the newly cleaned baby to its mother.

They'd never really discussed it, for many reasons, but mainly because they feared that too much preparation might jinx it.

"Let him come and then we'll decide," was his father's attitude. But Christina had secretly thought of it in between her many duties. She decided on Cornelius, after Auntie Maria's husband. A better substitute father she could never have hoped for.

Word of the new arrival travelled like the wind through the hills of Welgeval, and Maja came rushing over to verify it. He found Polomane working on the chairs outside. He had chosen a fairly strategic position from which he could hear the soft sounds of the crying baby inside. Kaatjie had locked him out while she attended to his wife, but wanting to be close to the house, Polomane decided not to go to the fields that day.

"Listen!" he said to Maja with pride. "That's my baby crying."

The pair stood with their ears to the window, listening to the gurgles and grunts of new life.

"*My vaderland!* Who would ever have …?" Maja exclaimed. "A brand new Moloto! We have certainly walked the distance."

"I know, I know," Polomane replied. "That sound is better than music to my heart. And who'd have thought it would be linked to me?"

Maja pulled up a small bench and sat down under the tree, while Polomane continued to sand the chairs.

"You won't believe what that woman Kaatjie said to me after she delivered the baby," Polomane said eventually, breaking the silence.

"What?" asked Maja.

"She said a man is not supposed to sleep in the same house as a newborn baby," Polomane said indignantly. "Where am I supposed to sleep? Under a tree?"

Indeed, now that they were settled, women like Kaatjie, who could still remember their traditions, felt that they should bring order to Welgeval and apply laws from their original villages where a newborn was protected by strict rules that limited contact. The only problem was that on Welgeval they lacked the means of enforcing them. Each family had only one hut or two rooms at best.

"You know Kaatjie," Maja reassured him. "She just likes to order people around."

Maja had noticed the busy young woman. She was always full of plans and strategies, much like himself.

"But tell me," Maja asked, "what have you named your baby?"

"Ah, names," said Polomane knowingly. "I'm not going to let you meddle with that this time."

"Come now," Maja pressed, "what's the baby's name?"

Polomane stood up. He had little time for one of Maja's lectures.

"I haven't decided yet," he said dismissively, looking towards the house. "But Christina has chosen the name Cornelius for him."

"Cornelius!" he exclaimed. "Who's Cornelius that you should name the child after him?"

"That's Christina's choice and you will have to talk to her," Polomane replied. "I accept it."

Polomane started walking towards the house, with his brother-in-law hot on his heels. He'd had enough of Maja's interference. It was time to establish boundaries.

"And now that I'm thinking about it," Polomane added, "I think I shall add my clan name just to restore what I've lost."

"But ..." Maja began. "Don't I ..."

"He'll be called Cornelius Malema Moloto, and you shall just have to accept it," Polomane declared.

Maja was happy for Christina and Polomane, but somehow he felt excluded. Borrowed happiness is not the same as one's own. He was used to leading as far as new things were concerned, so this reversal of roles did not suit him. On his way back home, he whipped up the idea of taking Kaatjie as his wife.

"Not bad," he said to himself.

Kaatjie would even give him a head start, as she already had two children. He took the idea to bed with him that evening, and the more he thought about it, the more he liked it. Kaatjie Mokwena was the sort of woman he appreciated: decisive and ready to tackle any challenge. She had arrived on Welgeval six months before, destitute and with two children in tow. After her husband had been killed on a hunting expedition, she was thrown off the farm where he worked. She'd scarcely been on Welgeval for half a year and already she was the person everybody depended on in an emergency.

Surely a woman like Kaatjie would appreciate a good husband, he concluded as he fell asleep.

23

A month later Gonin came back to Welgeval to hold a baptismal service for his daughter and for baby Cornelius. Christina and Polomane put on their Sunday best and presented their son before Gonin. It wasn't that long ago that they had stood in the exact same spot in the church, wearing the same outfits and listening to the same hymns, and already their clothes stretched tight across their chests and tummies. But even though they felt and looked like overstuffed sausages, they seemed to hold their heads far higher than when they got married.

After the service, the people of Welgeval gathered at Christina and Polomane's home for a party to introduce the baby to the community and to celebrate his baptism. A few women had stayed at home to make sure that lunch would be ready when the church service ended. Big pots of meat, pumpkin and *mieliepap* simmered on low coals, ready to be served. A table for the visitors, Gonin and Jenny, was laid inside the house, while the women put mats outside so that they could sit in the shade of the house.

When everybody had been served, the friends – Christina, Tsholofelo, Kaatjie and Maria – washed their hands and sat down to eat together from one large bowl.

From where they were sitting, they could see their houses dotted all along the western slopes of the farm on the other side of the river. Little footpaths snaked up to each door.

"*Mamokwena a ntsetse!*" Tsholofelo said in horror. "Do we really call those mounds of earth homes?"

"What is it now?" Kaatjie snapped anxiously at the ever-critical Tsholofelo.

"Just look at us *basadi* sitting here and eating like pigs in the dust," Tsholofelo remarked, scrunching up her nose. "Such exposure… how can we live and carry out our daily duties in the open air for all and sundry to see? No self-respecting woman should have a home without a courtyard."

Those little hovels dotted along the hills had seemed like the ultimate mansions when they first arrived at Welgeval, but now after a few months of freedom they could hear echoes of womanhood from their villages of origin: "How can a woman live like that?"

For a moment their focus shifted from their food to their houses.

"I agree with you, Tsholo, for a change," Kaatjie said. "Look at us here… all the monkeys in the hills are watching us graze like cattle in the veld."

Christina cleared her throat. She was beginning to feel personally attacked. *Why do these women see all these problems now, when I have invited them to be merry with me?* she thought.

"If you feel so strongly about it, why don't you do something about it?" she said sourly. "You can't come here and complain the whole time."

Tsholofelo had been a fully formed woman, with clear ideas on how a home should be run, when her chief had given her, along with a group of other girls, to the Boers as a trade-off to prevent future attacks. She had never been allowed to put her ideas into practice on the Boer farms, but now, here on Welgeval, where she could make her own decisions, she expected her home to have all the amenities she had been used to, especially a courtyard where she could do her chores in privacy.

"I'll call the first *letsema* so we can start building the courtyards for each other," Tsholofelo said.

"No," Christina snapped, "my house first, because that's where we made the agreement."

"All right, Christina, we'll start with you," Maria interrupted to neutralise the looming quarrel. "You have a baby, after all. I'll send my boys to collect cow dung tomorrow morning. We can start gathering the building rocks."

It took two weeks to erect the walls of the courtyard, using cow dung to hold the building mixture together. The women then dug the floor and levelled and compacted it so that it was ready for the final phase, during which they would smear the floor with cow dung to seal off the dust. This was the pinnacle of all their effort, where each one would get a chance to show her colours.

One week later, when the floor was dry, the women assembled in the courtyard, still clad in their long Boer dresses, ready to start sealing the floor. In ritual unison, each woman, with a big safety pin between her teeth, pulled up her top skirt and fastened it at the back with the pin. They then folded the underskirt so that it was just above their knees but still protecting their modesty while kneeling on the floor.

"Women, it is time now," Tsholofelo announced, brimming with the confidence of experience. "Who shall start?"

The question was already answered in her mind.

"I think the owner of the house should put her stamp on her home," Kaatjie said, challenging Christina.

"No, no, my friends, it does not work like that," Christina replied, anxious not to expose her ignorance of the art. "The oldest woman should bless my humble home with her unique pattern first."

"We can't spend the day trying to decide who should start," Tsholofelo said impatiently. "Hand me that piece of sack. I'll start!"

She knelt down on the piece of sack and placed a pile of dung before her. Her long legs, thin from their long stay under the big skirt, shivered a little from both exposure and excitement about the challenge at hand. She dipped her hand into a pot of water and took a small heap of dung, smearing it across an area as wide as her arm could reach. When it was evenly spread out, she paused a little to decide on her decorating pattern. Whatever pattern she chose would be the signature by which the women of Welgeval would recognise her from then on, so she had to think carefully. Women in her original village of Molepolole had so many interesting patterns – zigzags, small triangles and so forth – but her mother was known for the half-box style and, to honour her, Tsholofelo settled on that.

She extended her arm from the side and pulled the dung up, applying it and drawing four parallel lines with her fingers at the same time. When she reached the top, she turned across and pulled the same lines to the other side. She repeated this pattern inside the original half-box until it was filled with horizontal and vertical lines in descending order. Back and forth she went across the courtyard until there were three neat rows of box-style pattern.

"*My gonnas*, Tsholo!" Christina exclaimed, awestruck by the pattern and symphony of movements she had just observed. "Who can ever match that?"

"We'll see," Tsholofelo said, as she stood up to make way for the next woman.

"Who's next?" she called.

Kaatjie knelt down stiffly, uncertain of her plan. The only pattern she could remember was the zigzag one, and so, zig, zag, zig, zag, she proceeded below Tsholofelo's pattern, and after three rows her shoulder started to ache. She ambled off the floor for Christina to take over.

Christina was at a total loss as to what to do, but she was not going to let the others know. Because of her early abduction, she had no recollection of any of this activity in her village. But with her womanhood now at stake, she had to find a way. She decided to combine Tsholofelo's and Kaatjie's strokes, the long stroke with the zigzag movement.

Tsholofelo stared at Christina in disbelief. Never in her life had she seen such a messy style. Women in her village could always follow on the other's pattern with one that fitted perfectly. What she saw now was a real jumble – no rhythm at all!

What can I say? she thought. *We definitely come from different places.*

They took turns and repeated their patterns until sunset, when three quarters of the work was done.

"Women," Christina finally announced as she got off the floor. "Tomorrow's another day. The families have to eat."

The men took their cue from the women. They also clubbed together, helping one another to clear the fields with the plough that Gonin had bought from the neighbouring farmers. They planted maize in the large fields and, in the smaller ones, sweet potato seedlings, which the women had received as payment when they helped neighbouring farmers harvest their crops.

In the winter months, when the sun was too weak to grow anything and they were waiting for their crops to ripen, the men spent their time hunting, making furniture or *karos* blankets. The women also occupied themselves with various home activities. Those who had collected scraps of material from the peddlers who passed through Welgeval busied themselves with making *laslappie* blankets – large patchwork cloths. For others, this was a time for making clay pots.

Stashed deep in the flanks of Welgeval's little stream was clay so pure and precious that the women often wondered if it wasn't the same clay that God had used to create human beings. It never disappointed, obeying all instructions for the desired size of pot. It baked slowly and evenly, never cracking.

The women made pots of all sizes and for various purposes: small ones for drawing water from the river, middle-sized ones for keeping water in the homes, and large round drums for making beer. The beer pots were especially popular with the women in the nearby villages, who needed them to brew beer for special feasts, such as weddings. They were thus valuable for bartering.

At the end of the July month, just before the spring rains, Welgeval erupted into a new communal hive of activity. Their produce was ready, and there was more than enough for home use. Polomane borrowed a dozen oxen and an ox-wagon from a neighbouring farmer in return for help during the ploughing season, and the Welgevalers loaded the wagon with their extra produce. The wagon teemed with maize-filled beer pots kept in place by piles of yellow sweet potatoes, each the size of a child's head. In between the pots and the sweet potatoes, the women's brightly coloured headscarves stuck out; they snuggled in to keep themselves warm on their trip around the villages.

The wagon groaned out of the farm with the shrill ululation of the remaining women ringing across the hills, children and dogs running and yapping after the departing group of traders.

"*Haak! Haak, Slangvel!*" the driver shouted as he cracked the whip.

Two weeks later, a much lighter and more brisk wagon returned, with women holding on to an array of squealing piglets and chickens. The people of Welgeval began to accumulate livestock, and each year there was an increase in the number of wagons that left to barter.

PART III

Be gentle gentle on my mind,
Please do be gentle,
soft;
do not crowd my mind
with studied images of my past;
let me feel it first:

NJABULO S NDEBELE
BE GENTLE

24

POLOMANE

A soft summer rain started to fall just after we went to bed. Hissing through the thatch, it lulled us into a sleep so deep that it should be made illegal for adults. It was the type of sleep that lets whole families burn to death in a house without ever waking up. A loud banging on the door startled me out of this sinful slumber.

Who could it be at this hour? I wondered as I went to open the door. It was David and Jonathan – my two younger sons. I couldn't believe it. It had always been such a business getting the two out of bed. What was so special about this morning?

"Pa!" they shouted into the morning air. "Come, it's time to go and brand the calves." They swiftly turned away from the door and ran down to the kraal.

I threw on my clothes and followed them. Christina was still fast asleep when I left. She was heavy with child and spent much time in bed these days. This pregnancy had not been easy for her, because her feet swelled so much.

When I arrived I saw the milk bucket with the white milk cloth tied around its mouth already standing under the tree near the kraal. All the milking had been done. The boys had already let the calves in and they were about to start branding them. Interesting…

Just as I walked in, David grabbed one of the calves and wrestled it to the ground, and Jonathan came rushing over with the branding iron.

"Be careful, Pa!" he shouted. "Stand aside."

Well, what do you know? Stand aside? Branding had always been my job, but today they had called me to show me that they had taken over. I was proud of them. After eighteen years on Welgeval, my life was full. Who would ever have thought that this was all possible one child and cow ago? I remember Maja laughing when I told him that I was going to build a kraal for that cow.

But the strange thing about children growing up is that it is also quite unsettling. I don't appreciate the rush they are in, always talking about doing this and that and going here and there. Their restlessness makes me uneasy. My eldest, Cornelius, used to be a steady and stable sort, but he has suddenly started spending more and more time away, working for the Boers on the surrounding farms. He says he wants to make money so he can get married. Nothing wrong with that, but it's the influence on the younger ones that I'm worried about. My wife tells me that David says he wants to be a *smous*, wandering from place to place selling goods. Now, can you believe that one of my sons would want to do something like that? He hasn't told me yet, and I can only hope it's because he isn't serious about it.

When the branding was done, I took the milk bucket and headed home for breakfast, while the boys went to the river for a quick swim. I was hoping to have time to discuss this restlessness with their mother. As I drew nearer home, I saw to my great annoyance that Christina was sitting with her friends in the courtyard having a very animated conversation.

"So damn early in the morning," I grumbled.

I managed to grunt a good morning as I passed the chattering women and went straight into the house to put down the milk. Christina followed me in and started to prepare my breakfast.

"Father," she said excitedly, "you won't believe the news the women are telling."

"You know, Christina," I replied sternly, "I don't like gossip, especially so early in the morning. All those busybodies out there should be looking after their families and not spreading scandal."

"Now listen, Pa," she continued, as though I hadn't said a word. "Apparently a stranger driving ten beautiful Afrikaner cattle arrived on Welgeval last night demanding to be allotted a piece of land. He wants to settle here."

"What?" I replied, taking a mouthful of food and trying not to look too interested. "Where does he come from?"

This was indeed curious. Newcomers were always a source of gossip, but this one seemed special. I for one did not take well to news of their arrival. Don't get me wrong: some of the people who have settled on Welgeval are really good and I like them. Take Daniel Mokoena and his wife Maria, for example – real salt of the earth. But if we aren't careful, the place would soon be overrun by all these foreigners.

"I'm not sure ..." Christina replied, giving me a knowing look as she walked towards the doorway, "... but I hear he's an immodest sort of man."

With this piece of bait she'd hooked my interest, and there was no way of hiding it.

"Wait, *vroumens*," I said, my mouth full of food, "why do you say that?"

"I hear ..." Christina whispered as she turned back, "... that he introduced himself as Ryk Kerneels Sefara."

"Ryk Kerneels," I sneered. "What sort of a person calls himself Ryk Kerneels?"

Just then the boys came into the house, Jonathan already telling his mother what had happened at the kraal as he entered the door. David did not say much about the morning, but the smile on his face showed that he was pleased with himself.

"You know, Mother," I heard David say, "Oubaas Mostert's son on the farm next to us says that he's going to be a *smous* and later open a shop in Rustenburg. He said I could go around with him for a while so I can learn from him before I start my own business."

"A *smous*?" Christina replied. "But who'll help your father with the cattle when you're gone?"

"I will," Jonathan jumped in.

I overheard this conversation just as I was picking up the ropes to go and inspan the oxen. That was it. I stormed right back in to put a stop to this nonsense once and for all.

"No son of mine will go gallivanting around the world like a wild animal!" I shouted as I entered the room. "We have enough to do here on the farm. Just stop with your mad dreams."

"Oh, Father," Christina intervened, "why do you get yourself all upset like that? The boy's only talking."

"Only talking, *my voet*!" I boomed. "I will not have that kind of talk in my house. You boys finish eating. We have to finish ploughing that field today."

The boys joined me in the field, but they worked in silence all day long, avoiding eye contact with me.

"I won't have any sulking here," I said, trying to coax them out of it, but they ignored me.

They continued with their sulk well into the evening, skulking away to have supper on their own, I think, to make an impression on their mother. They thought they could influence my decision by softening her heart, but I told her to ignore them, and we had our supper quietly inside. We finished up in silence and Christina started washing the dishes.

I thought I had her on my side in this matter, but I was wrong, because suddenly when she finished the dishes she turned around and said, "Really, Father, why do you get so angry at boys' innocent talk?"

"Innocent talk!" I responded. "*Vroumens*, you don't understand. This thing has been worrying me for some time now. I wanted to discuss it with you this morning if only your friends were not around."

"What has been worrying you?" she asked, genuinely bemused.

"The boys' ways – always rushing around doing this and that. I'm surprised they are even thinking about going off to sell things, as if they have nothing to keep them busy here."

"I don't understand why you are worrying about the boys rushing around," she said. "That's normal. They are not old like us."

"You really don't understand, Christina," I explained. "It's like they don't like their home. Why can't they be happy with things as they are, learning from me, doing things well instead of having all these wandering thoughts?"

"Father," she said gently, "the boys are growing up differently from us. For you, a home was the best thing that ever happened. They take it for granted. They want to try out other things. Please don't worry. David will always come back to help in spring when you plough and in winter when you harvest. Surely you can allow him to go out and sell things with Mostert's son in between these times. He'll soon want to marry, you know, so let him go and make some money for himself."

Christina was right. Perhaps I was just growing old, wanting things to stay the same. I wanted my sons to dig their roots here on Welgeval. It had been such a journey getting here.

"*Ag*, let's leave it," I said, making light of the topic. "Let's talk about the stranger, Ryk Kerneels."

Suddenly Christina's smile twisted into a grimace. She buckled down as a familiar pain tore through her. I called the boys to go and fetch the midwife – for the last time, I promised myself.

25

"Ryk Kerneels, I say, Rich Kerneels! What arrogance! That man will bring nothing but trouble to Welgeval," Polomane muttered to himself. He simply detested the man. It was a bright summery morning and Polomane's mind should have been on happier thoughts, but he'd left his home only to be greeted, again, by the sight of Kerneels waving at him from his field across the river.

"Good morning, son of Moloto!" the man shouted merrily.

Polomane ignored him.

"How is your morning?" Kerneels continued.

Still Polomane did not reply.

"I see, not good," he said. "I know, sometimes we wake up on the wrong side."

By some unpleasant coincidence, the two always seemed to get up and head for the fields at exactly the same time every day. Polomane tried leaving earlier and later, but each morning, without fail, the same animated sight greeted him.

Kerneels, on the other hand, frequently went out of his way in order to bump into Polomane. He was trying everything he could think of to soften up the man, but the more he tried, the more suspicious Polomane became.

After yet another stony greeting, he decided to change tack by winning Polomane over through Christina. That evening Kerneels made sure he finished work before him, and went home to pick up some eggs and vegetables to take to Polomane's household.

Such kindness – Christina was impressed. She invited him to sit in the courtyard with her, ordering Sara, their eldest daughter, to make them coffee.

Kerneels took the opportunity to bond with Christina, and he immediately launched into his life story. He explained how he had been abducted by a Boer from the outskirts of the village of Molepo in the north and sold in Rustenburg, laughing loudly as he described how scared they had been on the journey south. He laughed even louder when Christina told him that they had also come down to the western Transvaal in the same way. But suddenly he grew sombre when he told her about his mother, whom he'd left lying, bleeding, inside a cave where they had hidden from the Boers.

"It's all in the past now," Christina said reassuringly. "Look at how God has blessed us. We have our own families now."

"You are lucky you have a family," he replied. "I'm still on my own and life is very hard for a single man. But I'm not complaining. I know God will bless me soon."

"True ..." Christina replied.

Polomane walked in just as Sara was serving coffee. Of all the things he had hoped would never happen to him, finding Kerneels enjoying coffee at his home topped the list. He was livid.

"What are you doing here?" he erupted, dropping his ropes on the ground.

Kerneels stood up briskly and extended his arm.

"Greetings, Oubaas Moloto," he said.

Polomane ignored the hand and turned to his wife.

"Christina, what's this man doing here?" he repeated.

"Father, that's no way to speak to visitors. What's wrong with you?" Christina replied. "This man is your compatriot and you are so unfriendly to him."

Just then Maja arrived and greeted the party, oblivious to the situation.

"Good morning, *swaer*! I see you've made acquaintance with our new resident."

"Hmph," Polomane grunted, disgusted by Maja's friendliness towards the stranger. He picked up his ropes to go and put them away.

Maja sat down and listened to the story of Kerneels's abduction.

"Did you also have your name changed?" he asked.

"Many times. I'm on my third, which I got from a very kind master who I was with before I came here."

"So what was your original name?" Maja asked.

"Lesiba of the Sefara clan," he replied proudly.

"We've not come across any others from the Sefara clan, have we Christina?"

Before Christina could answer, Polomane returned, still in a bad mood, and cast a cloud over the party.

"Can you believe it, *swaer*," Maja said excitedly, "Sefara here says we might have been together in the queue when we were booked in as youths."

Polomane did not reply. He just glared at Kerneels's handlebar moustache and flat nose. He reminded him of a billy goat. *How can such an ugly man be so arrogant?* he wondered.

Kerneels was younger than Polomane, so his arrogance or confidence, depending on how you looked at it, irked him even more. He'd always associated this kind of character with crookedness. Kerneels was also much shorter, and from where he was sitting Polomane could see the top of his head and the thinning patch towards the back. *Is that why he wears a blanket over his mouth?* he thought to himself. Like Polomane, Kerneels held up his trousers with both a pair of braces and a belt, but they were hoisted up so high that a shirt hardly seemed necessary.

"I must say, Bakone," Kerneels sighed, ignoring Polomane's unfriendliness, "we've come a long way."

Just then Sara walked in to pick up the coffee cups and clear the table. She was now sixteen years old and had grown into a beautiful young woman. Kerneels took the opportunity to illustrate his point.

"Just look at how blessed we are," he said, pointing to Sara. "She more than makes up for all the *stront* we went through."

"Enough!" Polomane shouted, rushing forward to grab Kerneels by the throat. "You say that again and I'll break every bone in your body."

Sara dashed away from the flurry of action, while Maja and Christina jumped to their feet.

"Just leave my house," Polomane boomed, "and never set foot in here again!"

Kerneels held up his hands to convey his innocence. "I'm sorry you took that so badly," he said, shaking his head, "but it was meant to be a compliment. You really are a hot-blooded man."

He stood up and turned to bid the party farewell.

"We shall be friends soon, I promise," he said as a parting shot.

Kerneels departed, but Christina, Maja and Polomane continued sitting and talking in the courtyard.

"Maja," Polomane fumed, "do you really know what you are doing, letting this man stay on the farm? He is trouble, my friend, trouble."

"I agree, Father," Christina said disappointedly. "*Hy is onmanierlik.*"

The evening wore on and the three old friends talked long into the night. Kerneels's talk of Rustenburg had made them nostalgic, and they recalled the incredible tale of their existence. Then Maja told Polomane and Christina of his plans for the future. He had decided to go and join Gonin in Moruleng. He and Kaatjie had only had one son, and Maja expected that he would be off to explore the world shortly, leaving Maja alone on the farm.

"I want to go and help Gonin in his mission work as I used to," he explained.

"Now that does it," Polomane said, utterly bewildered. His day was getting worse and worse. "I'm not surprised that my sons want to go gallivanting. They get it from their uncle. What's this life coming to?"

"*Toe nou, swaer*," Maja replied. "I'm sure you can see that this would be the best thing for me under the circumstances."

"What are you talking about? My boys have always been ready to help you."

"I know," Maja said, "but I'm not a farmer at heart like you."

"Now I've heard it all!" Polomane exclaimed. "If you are not a farmer, what are you?"

"Can't you see that if I go to Moruleng, your children will have a place to stay when they want to go there to finish school?" Maja continued. "We should make sure that our children aren't denied the chance of an education. Don't you agree, Christina?"

Polomane could not believe just how cruel life could be sometimes. Since morning it had heaped one unpleasantness after another upon him. Without waiting for his wife's reply, he bade Christina and his brother-in-law goodnight and went to bed to forget.

In the meantime, Gonin's mission in Moruleng was thriving. Two young missionaries from the Cape had joined him, and the village was almost split between those who embraced Christianity and those who would not abandon their age-old beliefs for the traditions of strangers. Gonin still had to work the school programme around the parents' need for the children to help with domestic chores, especially in the summer months when ploughing had to be done, but the benefits of the missionaries' ways were slowly but surely making inroads in the village. A crop of young men had not only learnt to read and write, they had also been dispatched to surrounding villages to preach and teach.

Gonin, realising that his school in Moruleng could only provide primary school and basic missionary training, had made arrangements with the French missionaries in Lesotho to receive his students and provide further evangelist training. Once a year, a few proud parents sold cattle and grains for money to send their children to Basotholand, and at the end of the year they came back as heroes who had seen and experienced things that no ordinary villager could dream of.

A new class of people emerged as education transformed the commoner's status, lending it the authority and respectability previously reserved for royalty. However, to be educated was not only an expensive exercise, it was also very demanding. It took all of a young person's free time, and most dropped out halfway through primary school. Those who stayed on until the end received a double helping of respect – one for intelligence and one for endurance. The villagers' definition of valour was slowly stretched to include success in education.

Gonin noticed this increased interest in education, and it bothered him. To his mind, it was a distortion of his intentions. Although he appreciated the increasing enthusiasm for conversion and learning, he was also worried about the meaning the people were attaching to it. Conversion seemed to be the fashion rather than a matter of a change of heart. However, Gonin's concern was soon tempered by the thought of his early days in the mission: how he had never thought he would live to see the day when he had the luxury of complaining about the motives of his converts.

After his arrival in Moruleng, Gonin had to deal with the political tension between the Bakgatla tribe and the Boers. The constant conflict between the chief and the commandant general of the Transvaal Republic had exploded into a major confrontation.

The confrontation had deep roots. Just before the arrival of the Boers in the western Transvaal, Batswana tribes, including the Bakgatla of Chief Kgamanyane, were devastated in the war with Mzilikaze's warriors, a breakaway group from the Zulu tribe of King Shaka. The Batswana tribes could therefore offer very little resistance when the Boers arrived. Instead they made a pact with them to join forces and repulse Mzilikaze in return for land for the Boers to settle on. But, because of their different understanding of land ownership, this agreement would return to haunt the Bakgatla in ways they could never have imagined. For Chief Kgamanyane and his villagers, land was seen as communal property to be shared while one was alive; thus ownership ceased at death, and the focus was on communal survival. For the Boer, however, land was something entirely different. It represented individual wealth, which could be passed down from generation to generation; land was something to own and possess personally. And so the Boers took full advantage of the Bakgatla's offer, cutting themselves large tracts of land, measured by the distance a horse would ride in one direction, and then its perpendicular, without getting tired. Vast swathes of traditional tribal land were gobbled up in the process.

Gonin was then thrust into the middle of the dispute over the village of Moruleng. For six months his main activity was to act as a go-between for the chief and Kruger, who claimed ownership of the land on which the village of Moruleng stood. He insisted on payment for what he called "his" farm, Saulspoort. The tribe had to come up with a sum of £900 within three months, and if the payment was not made at the end of this period, he threatened to take back the farm and keep the deposit they had paid. While recognising the extortion in Kruger's demands, the chief decided to pay up, as he saw the threat of eviction looming with the increasing number of Boers in the Pilanesberg district. He instructed Gonin to negotiate the price with Kruger.

The tribe sold their cattle, any skins they had tanned, all their *karos* blankets, their grains – anything that was of value. A total sum of £360 was collected, but Kruger made no concession on the price. He took the deposit and wrote out a purchase agreement, which was to be fulfilled within three months.

Then it was discovered that Kruger's plan to sell Saulspoort contradicted the Transvaal government's plan to tax the villagers. The government realised that the villagers could not afford to pay tax and for the land at the same time, so they forbade the purchase of the land. Kruger immediately replaced the purchase contract with a rental contract. For the deposit they had paid, Kruger said they could rent the farm for a period of twenty years. Outraged, the chief instructed Gonin to intervene. After a furious spat, Kruger gave Gonin an ultimatum: If Gonin didn't like the way the Boers did business, then he should simply return to his home country, or if he was so very keen to buy the farm for the *kaffers,* then he should buy it for them – as he had done with Welgeval ...

To rescue his mission work and restore stability in the village, Gonin decided to buy the land in his name. Chief Kgamanyane insisted on his tribe's contribution. More cattle and grain were sold, and Gonin called for help from Jenny's family trust in Switzerland. A purchase contract was drawn up and, when all payment was made, ownership of the farm was transferred to Gonin. Kruger should have been a happy man. But that was not to be ...

Diamond mines had just been opened in Kimberley, and droves of prospectors came to settle in the town. Kruger saw in this an opportunity to feed the Diamond City. He decided to build a dam so that he could produce more crops than the rain could sustain.

He rustled up a number of men from the smaller villages in the surrounding area to dig up large boulders and roll them away for his dam. This proved too much for them; they disappeared, and the Bakgatla, hearing of this treatment of people, swore never to allow themselves to be used like oxen.

At the same time, Kruger, realising the state of his ever-diminishing workforce, demanded that Chief Kgamanyane dispatch thirty men to come and help dig his dam. Kgamanyane was flummoxed.

"How could the man expect me to force my people to go and do that kind of work for him?" he asked. He consulted his tribal counsel and Gonin, and they all agreed that it was an unreasonable order. Kgamanyane asked Gonin to write to Kruger to inform him of their feelings.

Incensed by the chief's refusal of his demand, Kruger rode to Moruleng with his lieutenants, guns blazing, ready to teach Kgamanyane a lesson and to extract the men himself. The chief and the villagers gathered at the *kgotla* to make sense of the spectacle.

Kruger ordered two of his lieutenants to bind the chief's hands and feet and tie him to wheels of the wagon, while the rest of his men had their guns cocked at the villagers. He then took his riding crop and flogged the chief, stopping only when he had drawn a good deal of blood. His men let off a volley of shots in the air and ordered the villagers to send workers, threatening to return if they didn't.

Such humiliation the chief could not live down. He and a fair number of his tribe left to go and settle in the British Protectorate of Bechuanaland. Gonin was torn between following the chief and staying on with the remaining people. But, because he felt relatively settled in Moruleng, he stayed.

After all these events, Gonin decided that it was ungrateful to nit-pick about the tribe's motives for education.

26

MAJA

I did leave Welgeval, much to my brother-in-law's annoyance. By the time I departed, we were not on speaking terms. He sent the boys to come and help me pack and load my belongings onto the wagon, just to appease Christina, who was concerned about the bad blood between us. But he personally wouldn't come anywhere near me. I went to bid them farewell, but he just mumbled something I couldn't catch.

The man is insane, I tell you. He hates the idea of anybody leaving Welgeval. He said he saw no reason for leaving a place where we were all happy and making a good living.

"It's all about wanting to live like a vagabond," he declared. He went on to blame me for David becoming a *smous* and selling his wares in the villages.

Can you believe it? Polomane didn't even like the fact that his eldest son Cornelius married a girl from outside Welgeval. He thinks that everything must simply stay and happen on the farm. He just doesn't appreciate that God made us for different purposes. Polomane is a farmer through and through, what some people call a man of the soil. His greatest satisfaction comes from handling animals and tending to the land. And to fulfil his role, God gave him a bunch of strapping lads to help him. What did God give me? Two girls and a younger son; surely this must tell you that I was not meant to be a farmer?

Farming will just be a means to my life, not my sole reason for living. I've always enjoyed working with Gonin and helping him in the mission. I tried to deny that for a while, but now that I'm older and less able to do all that hard work in the fields, I'm returning to what I love. The boys and girls of Moruleng have learnt to read and are also beginning to teach. I couldn't stay on Welgeval and let my daughters miss out on these new opportunities.

The more I think about it, the more convinced I am that God made two types of people: those whose lives are dedicated to the soil, like my brother-in-law, and whose role in life is to provide food for others; the other type are like the Levites in the Bible, whose lives are meant to enlighten the world, just like Gonin. You will recognise the two types even by the way they are built. The Levites are slight of build, not made for carrying loads at all, and their eyes are bright, like two lamps in the head, ideal for reading books. You will agree that I fall into this group, and my girls are the same. My brother-in-law and his sons, on the other hand, are as strong as Afrikaner bulls. Need I say more? The only exception in my brother-in-law's family is his youngest son, my namesake Stephanus. He inherited our build, and I promise you he will prove himself in education.

I enrolled the girls in Gonin's school as soon as I arrived in Moruleng, and I haven't regretted the decision on a single day. They took to the books like fish to water. Gonin could barely believe that girls could be so much cleverer than boys. I also immediately joined him and Isaiah with the church work. There are other young missionaries from the Cape helping with the school, so I'm not really suited to teaching as I used to on Welgeval. Gonin and I have resumed our trips to the villages to recruit more students for the school and to preach to their parents. These past few years have felt very right for me; I am doing what I was created to do.

I was in the middle of one of these trips one May morning when a messenger arrived with an urgent call from Polomane to come to Welgeval. Typically, he did not tell the boy what he needed me for, so I was quite anxious. My first thought was that Christina might be ill. Ever since she gave birth to the twins, Hannah and Stephanus, she has just not been well. Their birth was very difficult, and even now, so many years later, she has not regained her strength. In fact, she seems to be growing weaker by the day. I am worried about her.

But I needn't have worried; it wasn't Christina. Instead, the most unexpected piece of news awaited me on my arrival. Ryk Kerneels had somehow managed to win Polomane over and they were now very good friends – so much so that he had asked to marry Polomane's eldest daughter, Sara. Well, this was a real surprise, considering that the last time I saw them together Polomane was reaching for his neck. I heard that after I left, Kerneels had ingratiated himself with Polomane and made sure that he filled my place. Once he'd befriended the man, it was easy to persuade him to agree to his marriage to Sara. But I know Polomane well, and I think the main reason that Kerneels swayed my brother-in-law to this union was that he promised to settle with Sara on Welgeval.

I'd been summoned to discuss the issue of *magadi*. As Sara's uncle, I would need to decide on the issue of bride price. Polomane, Christina and I met in their *voorhuis* to decide how much *bogadi* we should ask for. That parents could discuss and negotiate *magadi* themselves was unheard of in my village of Moletji, but since we had no relatives on Welgeval, we did it all ourselves. In our discussions, I was reminded of how strange Polomane is. He was very reluctant to accept Kerneels's cattle, worrying that it would give him too much say in family matters. I think he could not trust Kerneels completely, so he came up with all sorts of ridiculous excuses. But after a while I convinced him that *magadi* seal relationships, and that he should look at Kerneels's cattle as assurance for Sara's children, in case something happened to him. On this basis, Polomane agreed to four heads of cattle.

The wedding itself provided another opportunity to observe a side of Polomane that I had not seen before. He was as amenable as the best of us. Normally, he doesn't make a fuss about things, but the way he carried on about his daughter's wedding was beyond my understanding. First, he sold one of his best cows so that Christina could go and buy a wedding dress in Rustenburg. Then he insisted on slaughtering a fully grown ox and sheep for the wedding feast. Very much unlike him, he insisted that people from the surrounding villages be invited. All this *gedoente*, I couldn't get my head around. He just seemed out of his mind. Maybe I shouldn't talk too much, because my daughters are soon going to be married. Who knows, I might just lose my wits like my brother-in-law.

The wedding was a huge affair. The Welgevalers ate themselves to a standstill. Kerneels basked in every bit of attention he got from the crowd. His moustache seemed to do a jig of its own as the bridal couple danced around with the singing group from Ramatshaba.

I stayed on after the wedding because it was the ploughing season. I'd never bothered to ask for a field from the chief in Moruleng, because I wanted to continue ploughing on Welgeval and maintain contact with my people there. Polomane and I decided that the boys should start ploughing my fields first while I was around, but they told me it was not necessary for me to stay, as they would do it anyway. I was very grateful for the offer, but I decided to stay on. It was good to spend time with my family.

Polomane and I spent a lot of time together, tanning leather for ropes and shoes in his backyard. I also got to see a lot of Christina, which I liked very much. She had lost a lot of weight and had developed a wracking cough, which would not respond to any medicine.

"Christina doesn't look too good," I said to Polomane one day.

"Ja," he replied, looking up from his work. "She doesn't look good at all. She coughs all the time, especially at night. It just saps her energy. I don't know what to do any more."

"I hear the Germans in Phokeng have all sorts of good remedies for chest problems," I suggested. "Have you tried them?"

Polomane was silent. He just stared at the courtyard wall as if he hadn't heard me.

"*Broer*," I said.

"Yes, yes, I have," he eventually replied. "Cornelius and I took her to see them last week. She has been taking their medicines since, but I haven't seen any improvement yet."

Polomane sat down against the wall, with his arms hanging limply at his side. He looked very worried, so I decided to change the subject.

"And how is our young businessman doing these days?" I asked brightly. "Does he still like the life of selling?"

"I know what you are leading up to," Polomane replied. "You want me to admit that I was wrong."

"No, no," I said teasingly, "I only wanted to know if ..."

"I know your clever questions by now," he quipped. "You know very well that David is doing fine – very well in fact."

"That's good," I replied.

"He owns more cattle than I could have dreamt of at his age. I was wrong indeed," he said, putting his work aside again. "Life has changed so much. There are all these new ways of making a living now. But I still think that one must make the best of where God has placed you. I don't like all this moving around."

"You're right. We should accept life's new ways," I said. "Our children are going to show us things we never could have imagined."

Just then, Christina called us for supper. The boys were ravenous from the day's work in the field and I was tired from all the inactivity.

I retired to the *buitehuis* as soon as had I finished eating. I must say, I was feeling a bit guilty. I had not missed home at all that week. I slept contentedly on the feather mattress, where Christina had prepared a bed for me. Every evening when she came in to check if I was comfortable, we spent much time conversing about the past and the future, about our children and how our parents had missed out on seeing them. She asked me why we had never tried to go back home and find our relatives. I was quite surprised to hear this from her. She'd always insisted that we should move forward and not spend our lives retracing our steps. Because Christina loved Welgeval as much as her husband, this question seemed really strange. But I felt closer to her than I ever had since we settled on Welgeval.

I was awoken by the usual *gevroetel* of the boys preparing for the day. Polomane and his boys always woke up at the second cock's crow. I never understood why he had to wake up that early. The boys coped with the ploughing without us. But then he is the kind of man who believes it's a sin to let the sun shine on your back while you are asleep. I think this is another difference between the two types of people God made. People who live by their wits need a lot of sleep to rest from all the thinking. Muscle men recover very quickly after a short sleep. They cannot wait to jump out of bed and get back to the soil.

Polomane had already prepared coffee when I got up. He poured a mug for Christina and went into their room to give it to her. Since her sickness, Polomane thought that morning coffee was the best he could do to make her happy for the day.

"Christina," I heard him call from the bedroom door, "coffee is ready."

There was no response.

"Christina, *vrou*," he repeated. "I said here's your coffee."

Nothing. The wind buffeted against the front door, but no sound emanated from the bedroom. Polomane walked inside and stood at the foot of their bed.

"Maja," he called, not wanting to draw any closer, "I think there's something wrong with Christina."

"What's wrong?" I asked.

"I don't know, she's just lying there," he answered. "Can you come and check what's wrong with her?"

I met Polomane walking backwards from their bedroom. He was clutching the mug tightly, visibly scared. I went into the darkened room and shook my sister.

"Christina, wake up!" I tried. "Your husband has brought a hot mug of coffee for you," I said.

Her head rolled towards me, her eyes shut.

I felt a mild panic grasp my chest.

"Christina," I stammered. "It's much too late to be so fast asleep."

I knew I was talking nonsense, but that was all I could manage to get out.

Polomane came in and held his hand over her nose. It then fell limply to his side as he sat down next to her on the bed. He held his head in both his hands and fell completely silent.

Christina, my sister, was dead.

Polomane sat like a statue next to his wife's body. Looking at him sitting there, stunned with grief, I felt something push through my own sadness and demand, *someone has to take care of all this*. I stood up and shook him.

"*Swaer*," I called, but he showed no sign of having heard me.

"*Broer*," I called again. Finally he dislodged his head from his arms, and two teardrops landed on his thigh.

Polomane stood up and left the room as I threw a blanket over Christina's body. No one close to us had died on Welgeval, and although both Polomane and I had known a lot of pain in our lives, what we felt now was of a totally different breed. It was hot and searing, unmitigated by the fact that we shared it. I didn't think we'd ever survive it.

We sat next to each other in silence on top of the courtyard wall and stared at the equally mute Welgeval landscape. After a while Polomane instructed me to call the children and tell them what had happened.

27

Christina's grave stood lone under a young karee tree on the edge of the couple's first mielie field. A small mound of red soil, held together by rocks collected from the hill next to their house, marked her final resting place. In winter, when the veld was bare, the crimson rise in the land was all that one could see from the *voorhuis* window.

After the funeral, Polomane avoided that side of their house for a while, even though the stoep had been his favourite place for having his first cup of coffee. It wasn't because of what he felt when he saw the grave; it was his numb heart that couldn't produce the right kind of feelings towards it. It seemed that after having pumped happy blood for so long, it was simply paralysed with sadness.

Polomane allowed himself no time to grieve. He resumed his daily routine the day after Christina's death and worked even harder than usual. It was a technique he had used on the Boer farms, numbing pain with fatigue, and he found, all these years later, that it served him well again. He was left with five children still living at home: David, Jonathan, little Christina and the twins. Sara, now married, was worried about her father's increasing silence and his ability to bring up the children on his own. She and Kerneels decided to ask him to allow them to raise the three younger children in their home.

They found Polomane busy in the backyard as usual, and after a few one-sided pleasantries, which characterised most communication with him of late, Sara had no choice but to announce the purpose of her visit.

"Pa," she said softly, "David told me that he would like to get married soon. Has he told you?"

"No," Polomane replied briskly.

"Well, he said he hopes to do so in the month of May, just before the harvest," she continued. "I think, Pa, that it's going to be difficult for you to look after the children once he's gone."

"And how do you know that?" Polomane replied coldly.

Sara stood there awkwardly, unable to give an answer.

"Has anything happened to my hands or my mind that I can't do the things I've always done?" he boomed. "What are you here for, Sara? Tell me straight."

Sara felt the edge in her father's tone. She knew how it could explode into something quite unpleasant, so she stopped to search for more appropriate words. Kerneels decided to come to his wife's aid.

"Ja, Pa," he said in a casual tone. "It's just that I think we could relieve you by taking the girls to live with us. Sara could bring them up like a mother."

Polomane dropped the leather scraper he was working with and turned around to face Kerneels, his eyebrows pulled so closely together they almost touched.

"Who are you to tell me what to do with my children?" he thundered. "This is the kind of interference I've always wanted to avoid. You can take your cattle now if you think they give you the right to meddle in my affairs. Do you hear me, Kerneels?"

"Pa, you are taking it all wrong," Sara pleaded.

"*Ek vat niks*," he hissed. "Nothing at all. Kerneels, just take your wife and leave my house. I can't bear your gall to come here and give me instructions."

"But, Pa, we were only trying to help!" Sara said.

"Who asked for your help? Just leave me alone."

Sara realised there was absolutely nothing more to be said at this point. As she walked out the front gate it occurred to her that there was only one person who could help to resolve the situation: Maja.

Maja and Kaatjie had also been pondering what to do about the children Christina had left behind. They also knew that one false move could put them beyond the pale as far as Polomane was concerned, and so they had to think very carefully about how they would introduce the subject. David had already come to tell them of his intention to marry a girl from Ramatshaba, so this could be a good opening for their discussion about the future of the children. In a remarkable change of sentiment, Polomane was now intensely proud of David's achievements. His marriage plans might indeed be a pleasant opening to the more difficult discussion.

As expected, Polomane summoned Maja and Kaatjie to Welgeval to discuss David's intention to marry. Polomane felt that he had worked hard enough and could now settle down. Maja decided to strike while Polomane's mood was still favourable.

"*Swaer*," he began, sitting back in his chair, "I don't know what you feel about this, but I think it would be a real pity if all your children missed out on the opportunities for getting an education."

"Moloto, what are you talking about now?" Polomane asked, preparing himself for a verbal tug of war.

"Well," Maja continued, "I was just thinking that since you've done so well on the farm, it would be quite easy for you to pay school fees for one of your children."

"And why would I want to do that?" Polomane grunted.

Maja recognised the storm on the horizon. He jumped in quickly to deflect it.

"You know, our Martha has done very well at school," he pointed out, appealing to Polomane's competitive spirit. "She will be training to be a teacher when she finishes school this year."

"And your point is?" Polomane refused to take the bait.

"It is just that Gonin is even talking of sending her to come and teach here on Welgeval," Maja explained. "I really think one of your boys should have this chance."

Maja knew that any talk of Welgeval and the possibility of permanent settlement on the part of Polomane's offspring would carry much weight with his brother-in-law.

"I have to discuss your suggestion with Cornelius and David."

"I'm sure they'll like it," Maja said. "Young Stephanus looks like a keen learner to me."

"Do you think so?" Polomane enquired. The possibility had never occurred to him before.

"Ja," Maja confirmed, "those big eyes tell me there is a good brain behind them."

"Yes, perhaps you're right ..." Polomane warmed to the idea. "He does seem clever."

"The boy could stay with us and enrol at Gonin's school in Moruleng," Kaatjie suggested.

Polomane leant back in his chair and pondered. Eventually he said, "I think I like the idea. We can't be completely left out of this new order. I think Stephanus should go and stay with you and get to know his namesake better."

"Er ... and regarding the girls ...?" Kaatjie stammered.

But, before Polomane could reply, Maja pulled her from behind and whispered, "Don't push your luck, *vroumens*."

Young Stephanus left Welgeval after his brother David's wedding and was immediately enrolled at the school in Moruleng. The girls continued to stay with their father, and, to show everybody that he could do a good job looking after them, Polomane took time to supervise their cooking and other household chores. But Sara and the women of Welgeval were not impressed. "There's more to a woman's life than just cooking," they retorted. "What does he know about women's things?" They vowed to bring a woman's hand to the upbringing of the girls.

Maria Mokoena, who had recently been widowed, was just the woman for the job. Like the rest of the people of Welgeval, Maria had spent most her life on Boer farms following her abduction with other boys and girls from the village of Molepolole in Bechuanaland. But she and her husband Daniel were hardly a year on Welgeval when tragedy struck. Daniel died of the recurring chest ailment that had caused his dismissal from the farm where he had worked. Sadly, the couple had never had children of their own.

Maria was a kind woman – always available to help wherever she was needed.

One day Sara paid her a visit to put forth her request that Maria go to help at her father's house.

"*Toe nou*, Sara," Maria responded, remembering Polomane's ill temper. "Your father will not like to have a stranger in his house."

"True, Auntie, he won't like it at first, but the girls will," Sara argued. "You and Ma were such friends; he'll find it difficult to be rude to you. Please, Auntie, the girls need you."

"Fine, I'll go and visit them tomorrow," she agreed. "But I'm not prepared to put up with any of your father's nonsense."

The following Sunday afternoon Maria prepared herself for her assignment. With her *borslyfie* pulled tight and her chest neat and flat, she put on her floral blouse and tucked it in between the pink-and-white-striped flannel *onderrok* and her black skirt. Then she threw on the sparkling white apron she had last worn at Malan's house. She ironed it out with her hands to flatten the pleats around the waist. Finally, she wound a matching white headscarf, which she had spent weeks bleaching in the sun to remove the white lettering, around her head. As she stepped out of the house, Maria picked up a few wild *laventel* leaves and crushed them on her arms, dabbing the leftover bits around her neck, and then strode confidently towards Polomane's house.

A few such visits later, Maria had eased her way into the position of Polomane's new wife.

28

STEPHANUS

After he moved to Moruleng, Uncle took to using his Christian name, Stephanus, instead of Maja, and with both of us sharing a name, a lot of confusion could have followed. Fortunately, he never does things in a simple way. He embellished his title by including the fact that he was from the mountains of Welgeval. "*Stephanus van die Berge*" he called himself. Later people just called him "*Ou Berg*". I suspect he took on his Christian name because he wants the people of Moruleng to know that he became a Christian long before they did. He's like that, my uncle: the name he uses always makes a statement. Father told me that he had made a big song and dance about reverting to his original name after they left the Boer farms.

The funny thing is that nobody in Moruleng ever called me Stephanus either. My family had always called me Faan for short, and so they did too. The name Stephanus then became a sort of family heirloom, used only on special occasions by important people like ministers and teachers.

I was happy that Father had agreed that I should come and join the big school here in Moruleng. Uncle said I should study hard and become a teacher like my cousin Martha. But lately he seems to have changed his mind. He says I should leave teaching to the girls and become a minister – just like Gonin. There is always the chance that he might change his mind again when he discovers a more interesting vocation, but it doesn't worry me: for now, I'm just happy to go to school where there are so many children.

The teachers are very proud of Martha, and Uncle can't stop boasting and telling everyone how he ignored the doomsayers who were trying to discourage him from sending her to school. People here believe that it is better to educate a boy, because a girl will only go and enrich another family when she gets married. But Uncle scoffed at this notion, saying, "She's my daughter, and I don't care where she takes her education. I just want to see her use her brain and show the world that it's not a disability to be a girl."

His only son is still small, so he's pleased to have me living here with him. I think he secretly hopes that I'll make up for the potential loss of investment in educating Martha.

"They've seen nothing yet," he always says. "Wait until they see what a Mokone boy can do."

I think the fact that I'm named after him makes him feel as though he has some sort of ownership over me. He feels entitled to push me into the way of life that he values but did not have the opportunity to take advantage of himself. Talk about living through your offspring! He's unapologetic about that. He believes that the younger generation should complete their fathers' dreams.

"Otherwise, why give birth?" he always says.

Sometimes in the evenings, when I am studying, he comes and asks me to tell him what I've learnt at school. I also have to show him my school marks – usually an unpleasant ordeal, as he can never understand why I get some things wrong. It really annoys him. He expects me to be top of the class every time.

"*Mokone ga a phalwe.* Never should you as a Mokone be beaten at anything!" he demands.

The smallest complaint from any of my teachers unleashes his wrath. The other day, when Meneer Brink told him I'd arrived late at school, he gave me such a thrashing, he nearly skinned me alive. I used to be able to run and get away from his beatings, but he's now come up with a new way of holding me down – one from which I can't escape. He gets me to bend down, and then he clips my neck between his knees and applies his *strop* on my bare bottom until it feels hot. Uncle won't tolerate anything that shames the name of Bakone among the teachers. It is tough living up to his expectations, but thankfully his strictness is mainly confined to school matters.

During the holidays I go home to Welgeval to rest. I really appreciate my times on the farm. I forget all about books and immerse myself completely in farming duties. It's not that Father isn't keen for me to learn. He just doesn't push as hard, because he doesn't quite see the value of education. All he ever asks me is, "Did you do well at school this time?" and I usually say yes.

"As long as you enjoy it, Faan, that's all right," he replies.

Sometimes I wish Uncle had the same attitude. But then again, he is often unmoved by mishaps on the farm that Father could kill you for. I suppose they balance each other out.

I am always amazed by how well Father and my brothers have done on the farm. When I went on holiday last time, I found they had bought two horses, and David had returned from one of his trips with two Lee-Metford rifles – for himself and Cornelius. They are so proud of the farm, they are even thinking of asking Meneer Gonin to let them buy it. Father agrees, because he feels that Gonin has limited interest in the farm. He only comes to Welgeval once in a while to fetch vegetables or serve communion in church.

My closest brother, Jonathan, has learnt to use David's rifle very well. Now and again David allows us to go hunting, because he knows Jonathan will always bring something back. I just marvel at how accurately Jonathan can shoot on the trot. Whenever I can, I do some target shooting. One of these days I want to give him the shock of his life by beating him at his own game.

Jonathan is really more like friend than a brother to me. We share so much, including our bedroom and blankets. We often even eat from the same dish. My other brothers, Cornelius and David, are so much older than me, they are almost like uncles. They have both taken over from Father in looking after me. David buys me all my clothes, while Cornelius always makes sure that there's a cow ready to sell for my schooling. I think they all like the idea of having a brother going to school, because they didn't get much of a chance.

But Jonathan has been behaving strangely lately. He's agitated and snappy. Last night I asked him if we could go hunting today, and he reacted out of character.

"Why should I?" he barked. "Go on your own!"

I couldn't believe it. He's normally a pleasant sort of bloke who's always ready for action. He does most of Father's farming jobs, which he likes very much. Since my older brothers left home, he's really like the head of the household. Sometimes, before harvest time, when they are still waiting for the crops to ripen, David lets him go along on his sales trips. He's been to many places – Krugersdorp, Rustenburg – but I think he changed after his last trip with David. He often speaks of the mines in Johannesburg – how people are making lots of money there. But every time our older brothers come to visit, he nags them about buying the farm.

I don't understand: all this talk about the mines and the anxiety about the farm don't go together. One evening I decided to get to the bottom of his unusual behaviour. It was a warm, muggy night, and although Father had said that with all the swallows drifting in the sky it would rain any minute, there was still no sign of a downpour, so Jonathan and I decided to sleep outside in the courtyard.

We were lying on our backs watching the sky, hoping to see a shooting star, something Jonathan was very keen on. He said Uncle had once told him that shooting stars announce the birth or death of a great chief. He was always looking out for them in the hope that he would be the first to receive this important news.

"Jonathan," I began, "why are you so anxious that we should buy the farm?"

"I like it," he replied curtly.

"*My gonnas*, who doesn't?" I said. "Just because we like the farm we don't go about looking like constipated porcupines. What's wrong with you, *jong*?"

He shot bolt upright in his bed. "Are you calling me a constipated porcupine? I'll *bliksem* you, *klein stront*!"

"I was just asking, *broer*," I muttered.

"You're getting too big for your boots," he went on. "Is it because of that school that you can't respect your elders? *Ek sal jou dik donder!*"

This was nasty. Jonathan could only use that kind of language because Father was inside. I wish he'd heard him.

Jonathan lay back again and stared intently at the sky. A small quarter-moon cast a dim light over us, and I was able to see his tight profile next to me. I let him cool down, but I remained determined to find out what was eating him up. I was sure that his mood would change if he saw a shooting star.

"*Ouboet*," I said, once I'd given the stars a chance to work their magic. "Why do you get angry so easily these days? I'm worried about you. All I want to know is what is bothering you."

Yes, the stars had calmed him down. Instead of erupting, he turned to me and said gently, "You know, Faan, you are still very young. If I told you all the things I know, you'd be scared to death."

"I'm not that young any more," I objected.

"I would just let it go if I were you," he said, turning away again. "Just sleep and leave me alone."

"Just one last thing," I said. "Do you want to go and work on the mines in Johannesburg?"

"Yes, if they take the farm, I will. I'm really considering it."

"Who's taking the farm?" I asked, jumping up from my blankets. "What do you mean, Jonathan? What have you heard? Now I won't be able to sleep. You've got to tell me. I promise I'll keep it to myself."

Jonathan was silent for a while. Then he sighed once again and finally told me what was worrying him. He explained how, for many years now, since before I was born, the Boers had been fighting to gain control of the land, and that even though the British won a war against them, the Boers were still determined to rule. Jonathan said that the last time he was in Rustenburg with David, he'd heard that a number of Boers were planning to take all the farms that were not occupied by white owners.

"This means that Welgeval will be taken as well," he said sadly. "Because Gonin doesn't live on it."

"What?" I couldn't believe what I was hearing. "Does Cornelius know about this?"

"Yes, he does. That's why he wants us to buy the farm."

"What will happen to us?" I asked. "Where will we go?"

Jonathan took a very deep breath and said, "Let me tell you something, little brother. Whoever tries to take this farm will have me to deal with. I swear I'm not going lie down and let them have their way."

Unlike me, Jonathan was tall and well built. He was even stronger than Father now. I believed him: there would be a corpse on the ground if ever anyone tried to wrest Welgeval from us, and I was fairly sure that it wouldn't be Jonathan's.

Damn it, I won't let my brother fight alone, I decided.

"I'll also fight to my last bit of strength for our farm," I said.

"Easy, young man," Jonathan retorted. "It's still Gonin's farm. We may not have any trouble."

I lay down again, feeling very worried about my bold decision to fight. I wasn't much of a fighter. I consoled myself with the thought that maybe Gonin would do something about it. Jonathan was right: we might not have to fight.

29

The bruised remnants of the Bakgatla tribe in Moruleng picked up the pieces and installed Mokae Pilane as their regent chief, to be answerable to Chief Kgamanyane from across the border in Bechuanaland. The skies blessed the decision, and it poured with rain in a way that had not been seen in a long time.

Young people from the surrounding villages slowly trickled back to Moruleng to study at Gonin's school, and many settled there, enlarging the pool of the Bakgatla tribe.

Gonin and his young missionary assistants went back to work, and his mission thrived, boosted by a second crop of qualified African evangelists who had just returned from Morija. They were immediately dispatched to work in the villages, and more missionary teachers were sent from the Cape.

The first two African women teachers qualified from Gonin's school the following year, and among them was Martha, Maja's eldest daughter.

"What did I tell them?" Maja said triumphantly. "In these things a girl is just as capable as a boy."

Gonin sent Martha to take over the school at Welgeval. His cup was flowing over with the harvest not only from his mission work, but also from his own personal life. His children were ready to go off and study in the Cape and further afield in Switzerland.

The bushveld rain roared throughout the night and the next morning, ceasing briefly at around ten o'clock. Women hurried through the respite to do their household chores and remove the weeds that were now choking their plants in the fields. But every day, like clockwork, the skies would burst open again in the afternoon, just when the women were about to go home and prepare the evening meals. They were constantly soaked, and soon enough they succumbed to illness. A few of them came down with a fever that wouldn't subside, even though they chewed the root of *serokolo* all the time. The fever spread through the village, affecting young and old. Even Jenny Gonin got it. People were surprised. She never got wet working in the fields and did not cook her meals outside. *How did she manage to get it?* they wondered.

Gonin took Jenny to the doctor in Rustenburg, and he was shocked to hear the diagnosis. Jenny had malaria, and there was an outbreak of the disease in the village. Gonin couldn't believe it. The western Transvaal was supposed to be one of the malaria-free regions of the country. He'd never heard of reports of malaria in this part of the land. The curses of the western Transvaal seemed never ending.

Children succumbed to the disease first. Gonin conducted funeral after funeral, and had to rush back home to take care of his wife in between. Only six days after she fell ill, Jenny died. Gonin was devastated. With so much work still to do, it made no sense that God should remove his essential support. After the funeral, he shut himself off for months, nursing his pain in private.

While Gonin was mourning the death of his wife, the Boers continued to put a squeeze on Africans in all of the villages, spreading anxiety about ownership of their land with the appointment of the location commission to investigate new laws of land occupation. The commission came up with a menacing recommendation for the people of Welgeval: that no landowner should have more than five African families living on one farm.

Faced with the potential loss of his farm and eviction of the people, Gonin was forced out of his depression to respond to the new law. He wrote to Kruger, pleading that the people of Welgeval be allowed to continue living there as they had no other homes, but Kruger was firm in his refusal: the law would be applied with no exceptions. Despite this, Gonin rode to Welgeval to reassure the people and remind them that God was in charge, and that they should therefore outwait Kruger's threats, as they had done before they arrived on the farm. He also informed them that he would deflect the eviction threat by handing the farm over to the Cape Synod so that it would no longer be considered his personal property.

Recharged by the challenges, Gonin went back to Moruleng to arrange for his next batch of trainee evangelists to go to Morija in Basotholand. Young Stephanus was included in this group. But while Gonin was struggling to stand up against the Boer Republic, they in turn were put under pressure by the *uitlanders* – foreigners working in the gold mines demanding franchise in return for the tax they paid to Kruger's government. Kruger and his government reserved the franchise for those who had fought for the Transvaal against the British. This meant that only the Boers could have a say in how the Transvaal was governed. With the scar from the recent Anglo-Boer War still itching, the Boers would not risk losing their independence again by giving foreigners the right to vote.

But, in between quarrels with the foreigners and their British masters, the Boers decided to increase their authority on the Africans by demanding more taxes. They tore up villages and attacked anyone who would not comply. In the west, the Bahurutshe village governed by Chief Ikalafeng was in flames because he had resisted the Boer attack, sending them running for safety to the little town of Zeerust. The Boers came back reinforced and decimated the village. Chief Maleboho in the northern Transvaal mounted a resistance that brought shame to a commando of two thousand Boers and their foreign recruits. For weeks they tried to destroy the chief's mountain stronghold and starve him and his people to death, but the chief held out, releasing snipers now and again to take out a few of the commando.

In spite of these sporadic defeats, the Boers continued to wring out taxes from the Africans and the settlers in the gold fields while denying them franchise. They appropriated land from the Africans, and held them in small and crowded reserves.

In 1899 the quarrel over franchise erupted into an open war between the two white tribes, the second Anglo-Boer War. For a while, the Africans of the Transvaal kept out of the war, biding their time. The British got the upper hand and forced the Boers to seek refuge in the western border of the Transvaal, close to the protectorate of Bechuanaland. Chief Lechoe, son of Kgamanyane – now enjoying the protection of the British in the protectorate – thanked his ancestors for the opportunity to avenge his father's mistreatment. He sent two of his trusted regiments to teach the Boers at the border a lesson. His subordinate tribe in Moruleng rose up in support and launched an attack from Pilanesberg. At every turn, young Bakgatla men took the opportunity to finish off all forms of Boer aggression with wild abandon.

30

STEPHANUS

A year away from home. Who ever thought I could survive it? I arrived in Johannesburg yesterday morning after a long journey from Maseru on all sorts of transport: horse cart, donkey cart and finally a mine lorry that fetches recruits from the Orange Free State. After languishing at the station from the small hours of the morning, I finally boarded the train to Rustenburg in the afternoon. I rushed for the window seat before anyone else could think of it and stuck half my body out of the window so that I could suck in the cool minty air of my country. Soon the train trundled out of the station, coughing and shrieking out a steamy announcement of its departure. In the distance, dark green hills rolled past slowly, while a variety of karee and thorn trees, with their bright yellow baubles, lined the railway track on both sides in a guard of honour to lead the train out.

The damp of the first spring rains still floated in the air, and bright green grass had already pushed its way through the soil, creating a lushness that I had missed so much in Basotholand, where bare brown mountains dominate the scene. I was happy to be home. I settled back into my seat and was soon fast asleep, certain that someone would wake me up when we arrived in Rustenburg.

Jonathan, my trusted taxi driver, met me at the station. He saw me leap out of the train and came running over to help me identify my luggage among the many bundles that had been thrown out before the owners took a leap. I could never understand why the carriage for African people was not allowed to stop at the platform. A shocking number of people must sprain or break their legs in this high jump off the train.

After so long, it was good to see Jonathan again, and he was equally excited. He gave me such a slap on my back it nearly knocked me down. I wanted to punch him around a bit as we always did, but then I remembered that I was now a qualified evangelist. We were warned when we left the college that, as young missionaries, we should always conduct ourselves with decorum. My schoolmates were also still around, so I had to button down. Jonathan noticed my subdued response.

"Are you all right, Faan?" he asked.

"I'm fine, just a little tired," I said, hating myself for lying. I swore quietly that I would make him stop the cart somewhere on the road so I could show him just how pleased I was to see him.

I was proud that I was qualified to go out there and preach the gospel, but I felt I wasn't ready yet to be posted in the villages. In Morija I'd met some students from the Cape, who told me of a Wesleyan mission school that takes you a step higher in general education. Lovedale, it was called. Our teacher also spoke highly of it, and encouraged us to go and study further if we could afford it. He believed that a preacher with a sound general education could do more for his church than one with limited knowledge. I felt young enough to be able to stash more education under my belt, and like my brother David I wanted to do something that other people had not done before – be a little different from the run-of-the-mill evangelist around Pilanesberg.

I asked the missionaries to help me apply for admission to Lovedale, hoping that Father would be willing to sell more cattle and maize to pay for my fees. Of course, I was prepared to spend a year at home working for the first year's fees. I did not tell anyone about my plans after I arrived home, thinking I should wait until I'd received the letter of admission. I worked very hard that summer and made sure that Father noticed. Once in a while I would ask to go to Matooster to check my mail.

On one such occasion, towards the end of the month of February, I stood in the crowd outside the little shop window where we collected our letters, waiting for my name to be called. This was the third time I'd come to check my mail, but today I had a special feeling across my shoulders, the kind of tightness that you get before you jump from a high place. I was convinced it was a sign that this would be my special day, and indeed it was.

"Stephanus Moloto!" the man behind the window called.

"I'm here, sir!" I replied.

From the back of the crowd, I saw my letter floating in the air, passing from hand to hand until it reached me. This was it! "Alice" was stamped over the postage stamps. I went round to the back of the shop to open it, away from the crowd.

"Dear Mr Moloto," it read. "I'm pleased to inform you that you have been admitted as a student to Lovedale College for the year 1897."

"*Yuuuu!*" I yelped, punching the air with my fist. I must have let out a blood-curdling scream, because two men came rushing over to find out what was going on.

"What is it, man?" one of them asked worriedly.

"Why are you screaming like that?" enquired the other. "On your own, for that matter?"

"Who's died?"

I pulled myself together and tried to explain the cause of my joy, but the men left, shaking their heads at my apparent lunacy. I rode home immediately, eager to break the news to my family. I went straight to Jonathan's place, but his wife told me that he'd left for Moruleng early that morning. Trust Jonathan to disappear just when you need him most! All these recent trips to Moruleng made no sense at all. The people of Welgeval hardly ever left the place, except when it was absolutely necessary. Now Jonathan was starting something quite new, of which Father would never approve.

I found Father and Ma Maria sitting outside in the courtyard, waiting for Hannah to finish cooking supper.

"What's chasing you, riding so fast?" Father asked.

Indeed I'd ridden home like the wind, exhilarated by the opportunity that was opening up for me. I hadn't thought about how I would tell Father, knowing just how he hates us leaving home. At first I wanted to blurt out the news immediately, but with Jonathan's mysterious trips to Moruleng, I didn't trust Father's mood. I wasn't sure how he would receive more news of someone else wanting to go and "gallivant", as he put it. One false move and my plans for Lovedale could go up in flames.

"Yes, that was a hard ride," I said. "I didn't want to miss supper."

This was the most miserable excuse I could ever have given. I was never a big eater and everybody knew that. Father gave me a quizzical look, but said nothing.

I decided to go and tell Uncle in Moruleng the next day. I gave Father another mangled reason for going and he didn't question it. I suppose he had been expecting me to go and give Uncle a report about my year in Morija.

I arrived around noon and, from a distance, I could see Uncle reading the Bible in his favourite spot, under the orange tree in the middle of the courtyard. His sight was obviously giving him a problem, because he was leaning back, with his hand extended far in front of him holding the Bible. As I got closer I saw a walking stick lying next to him. He seemed to have aged quite a lot in the year I'd been away.

"Well, what do you know," he said, as I tied my horse to the tree. "My namesake in person!"

"Good morning, Uncle," I said, rushing up to shake his hand.

"*Môre, my seun*," he said. "I've been sitting here under this old tree wondering why I'm so tired this early in the morning. I always feel like this when I'm going to see someone I haven't seen in a long time."

"You mean I'd cast a spell over you?"

"Something like that," he said. "*My gonnas, jong*, bring that little bench and come and sit next to me. I want to hear everything about that cold country you come from. I hear it gets so cold there that babies' tears freeze on their cheeks. Is that true?"

"Now, that's an exaggeration if ever I heard one, Uncle," I laughed. I put the bench down beside him and took a seat.

"What's this?" I asked, pointing to the walking stick. "It looks like I left just in time or you wouldn't have been able to continue to enforce your rules like you used to."

"Don't you ever underestimate the power of the heart, son," he chuckled. "I've seen old men outrun young boys when their hearts have been sufficiently fired up."

I told Uncle about the land of Basotho, how men ride up and down the mountains on horseback, wearing grass hats and blankets tied tightly around their necks. For a long time we discussed my education and my year in Morija. Finally, I decided to break my main news.

"Uncle, have you heard of a college called Lovedale?" I asked.

"Never in my life, son," he replied. "Where is it?"

"It's very far, in the Cape. I've been admitted to go and study further there."

"Study further! I think you are going to be as educated as Gonin. I believe it!" Uncle exclaimed.

I didn't see my uncle pick up his stick but, before I knew it, there he was in front of me, doing the hunter's dance. Step this way; step that way – stick aloft, an imaginary spear in the air – Uncle danced.

"What did I tell them? *Tshaba Mokone*, be very careful!" he cried out. "Bakone walk the extra mile, son. Never forget that!"

Eventually, Uncle took his seat again, shaking his head and smiling with joy.

"So what does your father say?" he asked. "Is he as pleased?"

For a while I couldn't answer, as I was just wallowing in Uncle's happiness.

"He doesn't know yet," I said. "I thought he might not like the idea of me going away again, so you've got to go and smooth things out for me."

"*My maggies*, we'll definitely ride to Welgeval tomorrow morning," he replied. "We'll explain this modern world to your foolish old father. Don't you worry."

We then walked over to the mission to tell Reverend Gonin the good news. He was naturally very pleased. Two of his products, myself and another young man, were going to study at Lovedale. He promised to dedicate the next service to our safe travel to the Cape and success in our studies.

We went to bed early that night. I thought I would fall asleep immediately because I was tired from the long ride from Welgeval. Instead I tossed and turned, worried about how Uncle would break the news to Father. In his current excitement, the chances of him making a mess of it were great. I planned and rehearsed the correct opening statement and timing, but in the end I dozed off with the conclusion that timing was more important than what we were going to say. The moment had to be right.

Through some stroke of good fortune, the right moment presented itself shortly after my return to Welgeval. Cornelius's wife gave birth to a baby girl, my father's second grandchild. I couldn't have been more blessed. He would be as soft as a lamb.

A few weeks after the birth, Uncle was invited to the child's christening. Father was happier than he'd ever been. We all feasted on a big lunch that was especially prepared for the occasion, and in between mouthfuls Uncle sneaked in the possiblity of my going to study in the Cape.

"Mm," Father replied mid-bite. "Are you telling me Faan still wants to study?"

"Oh, yes," Uncle replied. "That's the thing nowadays. You have to fill your brain completely. His is only half-full now."

"Well, as long as he goes for that. I have to think of what I'm going to leave for the little one," he said, unperturbed.

You could have knocked me down with a feather – no fuss from the old man.

⸻

Two weeks before my departure for the Cape, the people of Welgeval were invited to Moruleng for our special service. They almost took over Gonin's church in its entirety. We sang lustily, Father included, proud to be made special on this particular day. Uncle and his friend, old Isaiah, sat next to the door to usher people in. They usually took turns to ring the church bell and usher in the congregation, but Uncle never liked sharing this responsibility. He wanted it to be his alone.

"I wonder why he can't pack it in. He's so old," he would say about Isaiah. Uncle wanted a niche for himself in church affairs. I was quite sympathetic towards Isaiah. After all, he had fulfilled this duty for many years before Uncle came over to Moruleng from Welgeval. I thought Uncle was being unfair.

However, and indeed if truth be told, my sympathy for Isaiah stemmed from ulterior motives. I couldn't have cared less about the silly argument between two old men. Isaiah had something that I really wanted: Elisa, his eldest daughter.

Elisa was a short woman, plump like a well-fed chicken. But all her friends looked up to her, especially after she quit her job at the Krugers. At some point her employers thought it fitting to start calling her "Arora, the female baboon". I hear that she just dumped what she was doing and told them she wouldn't let anyone call her an animal. Her employer was speechless. People bear all sorts of insults from their employers, so Elisa's strong stand was greatly admired.

She now leads the church choir, and every Sunday it is her distinct singing that starts up the hymns. Her voice is sweet, like warm honey – to me at least. I've heard some of my friends say that it is just ordinary, but I always make sure that I sit where I can get a full view of her. I like Elisa very much, but I am not too sure how she feels about me, and, with Lovedale on the horizon, I do not have much time to let her feelings unfold. The matter was becoming urgent, so I decided one Sunday that after the service I would declare myself and hope for the best.

I ran out of the door as soon as the preacher said amen and waited for her under the tree outside the entrance to the church. As soon as she walked past, I adopted a casual stride and fell into step with her.

"Elisa," I said, as we walked away from the church, "how wonderfully you sang today in church."

She smiled in response and my heart soared.

"I just wanted to let you know how much I enjoyed it."

"Thank you, my brother," she replied.

"I always enjoy your singing," I went on. "Maybe because this is my last Sunday here, I enjoyed it even more."

She stopped as we passed the church bell and faced me, hanging her head back a little. Then she gave me a smile so wide I felt sure that it would sustain me in the Cape. It filled me with the courage of a warrior and I knew I had to tell her.

"Elisa," I stammered, "I think you have moved my heart from its normal home."

Elisa's eyes seemed unsure of where to gaze. After looking from the left to the right and then left again, they finally settled on her feet.

"What do you mean?" she asked shyly.

My courage started to seep out of my chest and fear gradually replaced it. Elisa looked up at me for an answer.

Lord, let her be kind to me, I prayed.

"Elisa, you are a grown woman, you should understand how a woman can affect a man's heart," I pleaded. "I really shouldn't have to explain."

She dropped her gaze again and said nothing.

"Elisa, as a man about to go away for a while, I may not have the right to ask this of you, but I have ... I have no choice. I would like you to wait for me while I'm away studying. You see, I want to marry you as soon as I come back. Will you do that for me?"

Elisa kept her demure gaze on the ground while I was speaking, her face still, revealing nothing. But when I finished, I saw her pursing her lips and frowning – as if I had used the wrong words.

"Elisa, dear ..." I stammered.

She looked up and said, "How long would that be?"

"A year ... or two at the most."

She was quiet for a while, and then rather matter-of-factly stated, "I'll try."

31

STEPHANUS

I worked hard for six months to convince Father of my commitment to go to Lovedale. The wagon-loads that left Welgeval that year were all the produce of my sweat. He eventually agreed to sell two cows to send me to school, and Uncle also offered a cow for my upkeep at the college.

On the day of my departure I made arrangements with Jonathan to start very early in the morning so that he could drop me off in Derdepoort, a small town situated at the Transvaal border with Bechaunaland. With my old bag packed to the brim with blankets, clothes and whatever I could fit in it, I was ready to leave home once more – again for the period of a full year. I wrapped up the provisions that Ma Maria had prepared in a cloth and tied them to my hunting stick for easy carrying, and we were off. We arrived in Derdepoort at about five thirty on a cool summer morning.

I decided to cut across the veld to catch the train at the village of Mochudi in Bechuanaland. I sang as I strode along to scare off any animals. In between the fall of my footsteps, I could hear all the morning sounds of animals rousing. From the corner of my eye I saw a jackal walking a parallel path with me. It stopped when I stopped, the sly one, thinking I wouldn't notice it. I put down my suitcase and shouted and made a racket to scare him off. Jackals don't usually harm humans, but they can attract other, fiercer beasts. It ran off with its tail between its legs, but was soon back. I was tired of singing, so I decided to let him be. If I kept my eye on him, his actions would alert me to the presence of more dangerous animals. We walked along through the bush with occasional roars and yelps in the distance. Suddenly, the sky on my right was aflame with the blaze of the rising sun. I stopped and sat down on my suitcase, and I took a sip from my water bottle to welcome the day. When I turned to check, my friend the jackal had disappeared with the burst of sunlight.

I made my way slowly to the station and waited for the train. Two men who were going to the diamond mines in Kimberley joined me in my wait. The train soon arrived and I picked up my luggage excitedly. On closer inspection, my excitement diminished. I couldn't believe what I saw: a very long chain of open wagons carrying goods appeared. There was only one closed carriage on the train and it was reserved for white passengers only.

My friends and I were allocated one of the open carriages that did not carry any goods. It was the last open wagon on the train. Thankful that we could at least still continue on our journey, we threw our luggage in and scrambled up the walls of the wagon. To support our backs, we chose to sit against the sides of the wagon, the two men from Mochudi sitting opposite me. Because we were the last passengers and the only ones travelling in open carriages, the train took off as soon as we boarded. We spoke loudly to be heard over the noise of the wheels, but also because we were excited about the beginning of our adventure. Like me, they were breaking the mould, going off to work in a foreign place. They'd heard a lot about the promises of the mines from their relatives in Moruleng and couldn't wait to sample it themselves. They were heroes in their village for summoning the courage to take this journey into unknown territory.

The train moved at a speed slower than a man's walking pace.

We made bets to see by how much we could outpace it if we walked next to it.

"I could go as far as the engine," one man boasted.

"I doubt that," I quipped.

We took turns to walk alongside the train. Each of us had a chance to walk as far as one could go towards the front of the train without running. After ten minutes the remaining men in the wagon shouted for the runner to stop, and then came out and counted the number of trucks he had walked past. The winner got a piece of each man's lunch.

The exercise wore off our excitement enough to let us slide down and doze after lunch. When we arrived in Mafikeng the next morning, we jumped out of our wagon onto the platform to stretch our legs, but in no time at all a man carrying a little flag shooed us back into our *hok* like a bunch of stray goats. As we climbed back in, one of the men uttered a few words that would choke a preacher.

The train rumbled out of Mafikeng, and the sun beat down fiercely on us. The red-brown soil of Mochudi had given way to a limy white soil that reflected the shimmering heat of the sun. The whole countryside was so hot and dry I could see white dust covering the tiny leaves of the scrubby bush all around. All the way to Kimberley, we passed groups of scrawny cattle browsing on this scrub along the track. Our mood was now totally subdued. The man at the station had not been a good introduction to the people we were going to meet. My two friends lay back again, feigning sleep until it ultimately came.

I pulled out the Bible, the only book I had, and read. I went to the Psalms and repeated David's pleas for safekeeping. Then my mind drifted to Elisa. *Would she really wait?* I wondered. I had been stupid not to send my folks to pay part of *magadi* to enforce her wait. I turned to the Song of Solomon and let my heart soar with Elisa above the dust and scrub.

With the Bible on my chest I fell asleep and only woke up when the train arrived in Kimberley. My friends rubbed the sleep from their eyes, shook my hand and jumped down from the carriage. With their little bundles slung over their shoulders, they made their way into unknown futures. Fearing what had happened in Mafikeng, I elected to stay in the wagon.

I watched my friends disappear behind the station house. The station was crowded with white people moving up and down the platform, fetching their relatives from the train. No one got on to my wagon. It seemed I would have it to myself for the rest of the trip. We were on the station for thirty minutes or so when, at around five o'clock, the train lumbered out of the station. I remained standing against the wagon side so I could see the rest of the town of Kimberley and its surroundings. The town was situated quite far from the station, so all I could see was smoke from the houses, hovering in the windless sky. The countryside was as barren, flat and dry as that of Mafikeng, with the same limy soil. I walked around the wagon for some exercise and to work up an appetite for my solitary dinner.

With all this flat barrenness around me, I decided to settle down again and create my own entertainment. I had never been on my own for long periods of time, so the rest of this journey would be a new challenge for me. I made myself a comfortable nest with my blankets and continued reading the Bible, and when I grew tired I sang all the hymns and songs I could remember. That kept me busy until sunset. I then laid out my supper in front of me and enjoyed it in the soft moonlight. Two days into this journey and I was already finishing off the chicken. The *pap* was long gone. I was left with three pieces of dry meat and a bit of bread. I reckoned, with careful rationing, this would last me to the end of my trip.

As we travelled further from Kimberley, tufts of dark cloud

floated over the moon and cut off all the light. With my tummy full and my cosy corner beckoning, I saw no reason to stay up. I lay down to sleep, and my breathing took on the rhythm of the rattling train wheels. My mind dived down below the immediate noise and picked up the more ethereal sounds of sleep.

Suddenly, I felt Elisa's hand on my shoulder and heard her soft voice asking me, "Faan, do you really think I should spend all this time, two years you said, waiting for you to come back and marry me? Do you really think that it is fair?"

She was standing in front of me in her church choir uniform, very seriously waiting for my response. I reached out to touch her and plead my case, but my hand knocked over the suitcase next to me. I woke up at the thud of the falling case and sat up with my head on my knees, trying to formulate an answer to Elisa's question. For the first time I had doubts about the wisdom of this escapade to Lovedale. At what price would it be achieved? Was it really worth the sacrifice of life with my family, my ageing father and even the love of the woman I hoped to marry?

I stretched out my legs, put my hands on my lap and really faced myself for the first time. A cautious voice inside me said that all this was foolishness of major proportions. I had never met anyone from Lovedale. How could I invest two years of my life in this kind of uncertainty? I started to think of how I could reverse my stupidity – how I could go back home. But this train of thought drove me into a brick wall. What would I say to Father? That he sold his cattle to give me a ride on a train to Kimberley? And Uncle, what would I tell him? That I lacked the balls to see my dreams through? Forget it: I would rather die on a railway station platform than face the twin wrath of those two old men. I was soon fast asleep again, forcing myself to see beyond today.

I don't know how long I'd been asleep, but two drops of rain splattered on my face and woke me up. More drops followed, and I was soon in a torrent. My blankets and everything on and around me were soaking wet. I took off my shoes and tied them to a nail on the side of the wagon. I tried to scramble up to the top of the wall, but kept slipping. Finally, I succeeded in perching myself like a half-drowned sparrow on the ledge, with my suitcase on my lap. The train then screeched to a halt. We had reached a small town called Blearney, which I'd seen on the map. It wasn't too far from Alice, where I would finally alight. I thanked God for the opportunity to get on to dry land.

I jumped off as soon as the train stopped, hoping to get rid of all the water on me and stand in the sun for a while. I shook myself like a wet dog and hopped about to warm myself up a little. From out of nowhere, a blow to my head knocked me to the ground. I had not heard the railway policeman approaching.

"Get back to where you came from!" he shouted. "No *kaffers* are allowed on this platform!"

Tail between my wet legs, I clambered back into the wagon, and sat on the far-side wall. I watched white people strolling back and forth on the platform. *What does one man drying himself on a station platform take away from these people?* I wondered. Their cruelty seemed to be an end in itself.

At least it has stopped raining, I noted gratefully.

As I hung up my jacket and shirt to dry, I saw an ominous newspaper headline emblazoned across a poster on the platform: *Shoot Down the Church Bell*. It later became clear to me that the headline referred to growing white resistance to the missionary education of black people.

God, keep me safe, I prayed, as the train hurtled towards my final destination.

32

The war between the Boers and the British opened up the opportunity to settle a number of unofficial scores. By this time the Bakgatla had been granted permanent residence on the farm Saulspoort or in their village of Moruleng, but the situation with Welgeval remained uncertain. The people of Welgeval believed that it was the Bakgatla's assertiveness that had restored them to their land, which was a promising turn of events. In their own ordeal, however, they felt completely outnumbered and hindered by the knowledge that Welgeval was not really theirs to fight for.

Gonin wrote again to request a special dispensation for them, but the Republic authorities sent a curt "no", arguing that giving one native special treatment would open a floodgate of requests – no native would be allowed to live on private land, and that was that.

A definite eviction threat hung over the farm. Some of the Welgevalers decided to move to surrounding villages before a forced removal was carried out, but Polomane's family and a few others decided to sit it out and wait for the worst.

Jonathan felt compelled to do something about their security. He spent most of his waking moments planning and straining to find a way out of the trap. One day he decided he'd had enough. *This is it*, he said to himself. *Bakgatla are sitting pretty, their hearts are white with satisfaction over the vengeance they wrought on the Boers. The miserable creatures will never come back to torment them again. What about us, the people of Welgeval? Are we going to be forced back to the life of destitution that our parents came from? No way!*

I'm going to go in there to teach those Boer bastards that there are men living on Welgeval as well.

Jonathan couldn't share his plans with his brothers or any of the other men on Welgeval, as they did not share his sentiments. But his friends Modise and Molifi from Moruleng had missed out on the opportunity to be part of a regiment that attacked the Boers during the war because they were at cattle posts. They were itching for a chance to seek vengeance.

"Let's go and finish them off before they try to evict you," they said to Jonathan when he proposed attacking the Boers who were threatening Welgeval. The three believed that the threat emanated from the Boers around Kruger's farm in Boshoek, and, if they could suppress it there, Welgeval would be secure.

Jonathan borrowed horses for his friends and gave his wife an impassioned speech about the need to buy cattle at a cheap price while the Boers were unsettled.

"*My vrou*," he intoned, "our children are growing older. We must make sure we have money to send them to school when the time comes."

He predicted, correctly, that his wife would agree to any venture that supported the good of the children.

Very early the following morning, Jonathan rode quietly out of Welgeval, his wife looking on fondly. With his brother's Metford tucked away under the saddle, he and his friends rode furiously in the direction of Boshoek, stopping halfway to their destination at the Kgetleng River so that they could finalise their plan and let the horses drink.

They had just sat down when they heard the sound of approaching horses. It sounded like there were many riders, five at least – more than Jonathan and his friends. They grabbed their horses and hid them in a grove of trees along the banks of the river and then ran up towards the hills to hide in the burrows of the aardvark. In a panic, they chopped off dry branches from trees to cover the entrances of each of their hiding places so that the dens looked undisturbed.

Quietly they waited, hoping to hear the riders disappear in the distance, but the sound of hooves kept drawing nearer and nearer, and, as they approached, Jonathan detected the sounds of barking dogs in the background.

The sounds kept approaching, until a high-pitched yelp hurt his ears. The branches rustled above his head. A dog must have been nosing around right above him.

Jonathan held his breath, feeling faint in the earthy heat of the hole. A babble of voices thundered above ground, but in between the yelps of the dogs and the thuds of the horses' hooves he could not make out any individual words.

And then silence. They seemed to have moved on. They must have thought the dogs were barking because of the smell of the aardvark, Jonathan reasoned. In the dark, he released a quiet sigh and ran his fingers over David's Metford. A drop of sweat ran down the side of his temple. It got hotter.

Just then, a crunching sound crackled overhead and asphyxiating fumes billowed in from above. The men had lit the branches at the entrance and Jonathan was trapped. Choking and coughing, he leapt through the flames, gasping for breath and almost knocking down the man standing aiming his rifle at the entrance.

The man stepped back to get a clearer view of his prey.

"Is that you, Jonathan?" he blurted out, a flicker of recognition in his eyes. The Boer recognised him from the last cattle auction, where Jonathan's father had bought two calves from him. But before Jonathan could answer, he released two bullets, shooting him through his heart and stomach.

Molifi and Modise leapt out of their holes in the midst of the smoke and hail of bullets, but the men didn't shoot at them. Instead, they led them to the trees a little further away from the fires and took turns to beat them up, tossing them from one man to another until they grew tired.

"Now take that dead dog to its father," Jonathan's killer said to Modise and Molifi.

"Tell him that it was foolish to send his son to steal our cattle," another added, kicking Jonathan's body.

The Boers from around Boshoek had apparently formed groups to look out for, and deflect, any Bakgatla attackers. Spotting Jonathan and his friends riding towards Boshoek, they had followed them for a few miles before being noticed.

Against several dogs and six armed men on horseback, Jonathan, Molife and Modise and David's Metford stood no chance.

PART IV

The weeds run riot where our house is fallen
ourselves we roam
the wilderness
'Go tell them there across the seas go tell him'

ES'KIA MPHAHLELE
A POEM

33

STEPHANUS

I came back home after a year that seemed to drag on for much longer than any other in my life. And so much had changed. A few weeks before I left Lovedale, I received a letter from my eldest brother, Cornelius. It had taken two months to reach me, and I had just finished the English examination when the housemaster delivered it to me, opened and read of course. I noticed that he'd waited until I was on my own before giving it to me. I read it once and then folded it up quickly and placed it back in its envelope. Lacking the stomach to digest its contents, that Jonathan was dead, I shoved it into the bottom of my suitcase under my bed.

A week before "home go", with so much excitement in the air, the boys were taking longer and longer to be quiet and fall asleep after "lights out". Most of us had been confined to Alice, even during the winter vacation, because we couldn't afford to go home and come back again. I stayed awake the longest – not because I was excited, but because after dark my mind lifted the shutters on the room in which that piece of bad news was stored. At first it was so scary I couldn't face it, so I immediately pulled down the shutters again. But with this daily exposure, my courage grew. Still, I couldn't believe it. I decided to put it back in storage, hoping that it would be proved wrong when I got home. Death had so far been a total stranger in my life. My mother had died when I was still too young to register her loss in any significant way.

By the time I finished my exams, I was feeling completely detached from the news, and I boarded the train to Kimberley convinced that Cornelius had made a mistake. I caught my train to Mochudi from Kimberley, excited and looking forward to seeing Jonathan at the station.

When we arrived at Mochudi station, I stretched half my body out of the window and searched for Jonathan among the many men standing atop their mule carts, waiting to spot their relatives as they jumped off the train. Jonathan's size usually helped me to distinguish him from the masses.

He wasn't there.

I scanned the men waiting next to their carts on the ground, hoping Jonathan had changed his style, but instead of him I saw Nelie's eldest son, David, waiting. My alarm bells rang. Jonathan had never missed an opportunity to fetch me from any station. I leapt from the train and picked up my luggage – without help from my nephew, as he was new to this ritual of fetching somebody from the station. When I finally straightened up and walked towards the cart, reality struck and broke my heart into splinters.

Men in my family don't show weakness in public, but I couldn't help clinging to David, there and then, and sobbing my eyes out. I was utterly devastated.

I think David was quite embarrassed by the scene I was causing, because he gently but firmly pushed me away. I pulled myself together, enough to get into the buggy, and then started sobbing again. I'm not sure when or why I stopped, but somehow at some point the tears ceased to flow. I then plunged into an abyss of sadness from which I saw no way out. For two weeks back on Welgeval, this hellhole was my home. Managing only a grunt now and again, I did very little and spoke to no one.

Tired of my brooding, Father snapped one day.

"Enough of this, Faan," he chided. "Stop lying around like a sack of mielies. There's more pain from where that one came. I want you to drive me to church for *nagmaal* on Sunday."

We set off for Moruleng at about five o'clock on a Sunday morning. I hadn't been up so early since my return, and the cool breezy air and the regular clomping of the horses' hooves on the gravel road released a warm balm in my chest. I felt the ice at the bottom of my heart begin to melt and my mind skipping from one thought to another, something it hadn't done in a long time. Finally, it settled on one thing, and the more I thought about it, the more the heaviness I'd lived with for so long lifted until my face stretched into a smile: Elisa.

Did she wait for me? I dared to wonder.

I still lacked the strength to grow anxious about the answer, but I held on to the thought, and only once allowed my imagination to venture into what it would feel like to see her again. What a strain!

I took my place in the church almost instinctively, and as always positioned myself so that I would have a direct view of Elisa as she led the choir. I couldn't believe it! The second I set eyes on her, my heart began to flap around like a wanton maiden. I looked away to keep myself calm, but the strain was too severe. When I glanced at her again, I was suddenly desperate to know: Did Elisa wait for me?

After the service I caught up with her near the bell at the exact spot where I'd asked her to wait. I had to find out.

"Oh, Faan, I heard about your brother," she said as soon as she saw me. "It's really sad."

"Thank you, Elisa," I replied. "Words can't describe how I feel. Still, it's very nice to see you again."

I grabbed her hand and shook it rather too long. I looked her straight in the eye, hoping to draw out the answer to my burning question. It was really good to see Elisa again, and my heart agreed.

It was airy and light, completely devoid of yesterday's sorrows. Suddenly, she pulled her hand free.

"How have you been, Elisa?" I asked, taking her hand back again.

"Very well, Faan, but I couldn't wait for your return."

"What do you mean, you did not wait?" I asked anxiously, hoping that my ears were playing tricks on me.

"It was hard," she said, again retrieving her hand. "All my friends kept telling me how stupid I was to wait for someone who would meet interesting girls in the Cape."

"Elisa, what are you saying?" I said in utter panic.

"Well, I told them I'd take my chances," she said, finally looking me in the eye.

"Now tell me slowly, Elisa," I said sternly. "Did you wait for me, *skattie*?"

"Yes, Faan. It was hard, but I did. We can finally make decisions about our future."

I thought I was acquainted with all the feelings of which my heart is capable, but this one was a totally new experience. The shameless maiden broke into unabashed *bollemakiesies*, showing her naked thighs in public! The sudden switch of emotions was too much for my knees. I felt them wobble.

Pull yourself together, I scolded myself, ashamed to reward Elisa's courage with such weakness. I stood up straight to appreciate her commitment to me, and then the idea that we serve a fair God suddenly made sense: He took with one hand and gave with another.

I immediately informed Father and Uncle of my desire to marry Elisa, a little disappointed that I couldn't go back to Lovedale to do matriculation. But I couldn't risk losing her again. To ease my conscience, I vowed to myself, on my mother's and brother's graves, that Elisa and I would bear a son who'd take care of matric for me.

Land of My Ancestors

My family fetched Elisa from her home in the ceremonious style that she desired. She would have none of the slow-moving ox-wagon to take her to her new abode. Uncle and my brothers fetched her in a cart drawn by two of our best horses. There would be no mules for this journey.

The wedding party arrived on Welgeval at dawn, before anybody started moving about. A new bride was a treasure covered with mystique until she was officially unveiled at the reception party. But a few early-rising women who were fetching water from the well heard the horses strut the path to my parents' house, and broke into a spontaneous ululation, which reverberated across the hills. Father came out of the house with his Metford and shook the morning further with a few rounds in the air, while Ma Maria fussed about the preparations for the feast. I smiled with pride from my bedroom. This was the best day of my life.

⚭

We settled down in the small cottage that Father had helped me build, and I took up a teaching post at the local school. Soon Elisa was expecting our first child, and I was the happiest man this side of heaven.

Uncle was extremely proud, not only because there was now a third generation of Molotos, but also because of what he called "the steady ascent of the Levites of the Moloto clan to their rightful positions". I was the second of the educated Molotos and had taken over the school from my cousin Martha, who, after her first husband's death, had remarried to Chief Ramono Pilane in Moruleng.

Father, on the other hand, was simply pleased that I was back on the farm and due to deliver him his last batch of grandchildren.

But death visited my new family early. My firstborn arrived tired, as my people say.

Father and all my relatives consoled us and said that as long as Elisa and I were together, there was still hope for more. I never thought this hope would go through so much testing. My second child was also stillborn. At this point my faith was shaken, not understanding why God would want to frustrate our love so much. Thankfully, our third survived. With renewed hope we named her Gadifele, which translates as "God's gifts never end".

Soon Gadifele had a sister, a lusty girl, whom I named Christina, after my mother. We lost two more children after her, but in August 1910 were blessed with my only son, whom I named David Polomane, after Father. I felt not only consoled, but very happy as well. A son crowns the father's head.

The year 1912 started just like any other, but it was also different in that Welgeval had recently gone through one of a few good rainy seasons. The veld wore a thick carpet of green, and the little stream gurgled across the farm. With all this lushness, our potbellied cattle's coats gleamed.

We were just getting used to this year of plenty when word came from the Cape, where Gonin had gone on sick leave, informing us that he had died.

The news was a shock to all of us. Gonin had been such an important part of our lives. We almost believed he would always be around. Even though Father and Uncle never talked much about how they had met him, there was always an abiding sense of gratitude to Gonin. I felt particularly grateful to him because he had arranged a scholarship for me when I went to Lovedale so that Father only had to pay for living expenses. Father and Uncle said Gonin's death marked a change of guard, and that it wouldn't be long before they followed.

"That's the first bell," Father announced solemnly. "I've been wondering which one of the three of us would be the first to go. That man Gonin has lived his allotted years fully and he's done a lot of good work. We thank God for his life."

Much to our disappointment, Gonin was buried in the Cape and none of us could attend the funeral. Soon after, his son appointed a lawyer named Van Velden to administer his father's estate. We were more than pleased to learn that Gonin had offered the people of Welgeval first option to buy the farm. The news came in good time, because Pretoria had been busy preparing the 1913 Land Act – a law that would force Africans off most of their land, especially privately owned land. The Land Act decreed squeezing all of the native inhabitants of the country into reserves that formed a mere thirteen per cent of the total land surface. We were constantly worried about our continued stay on the farm. Cornelius jumped at this offer and asked Father to call a meeting of his relatives to discuss our response. There really wasn't much to discuss – we just had to agree on how we would meet the stipulated terms of payment.

Van Velden said the farm would cost us a total of £2 408, and we agreed to put down an immediate deposit of £548. The balance of £1 860 was to be paid off at a rate of £372 per year. He also told us that Gonin had specifically instructed that we should not be charged any interest on the balance.

Luckily, we had had two good rainy years, and our animals were in excellent shape to fetch good money at the auction. Each of the original nine families on Welgeval sold their cattle to make up the required deposit. Chief Ramono Pilane, now Uncle's son-in-law, was invited to join the buying group and put down some money as well.

This newfound security sat well on our shoulders. We had no doubt that we would make the rest of the payments. And so, on 27th June 1912, ownership of the farm Welgeval was officially transferred to us.

But alongside these happy events, Elisa and I bore two more trials of stillborn children. We had lost six children in all when ultimately God blessed us with our last daughter, whom we decided to name Madira, after Elisa's great-aunt who lived in Lesotho. It was believed that a far-fetched name like that would shock the local jinx and give her a fighting chance to live.

34

Every year the people of Welgeval prepared themselves to make their annual instalment to Gonin's estate, and Stephanus took on the role of collecting the money and delivering it to Van Velden in Rustenburg. Imbued with the pride of ownership, life on the farm seemed to roll on more smoothly than ever. Even the summer rains came dot on time, soaking the earth until it was a mass of sweet grass. Welgeval yielded its products from a generous heart, and the wagons that left the farm every winter groaned with the weight of their ever-heavier loads. All the children were enrolled in the school, and there was still spare money to build a proper church and school building.

In these conditions, one would have expected the average Welgevaler to settle down and wallow in this most unusual life of ease, but instead a strange restlessness developed. More young men and women enrolled at the mission boarding school in Moruleng, while some ventured further afield for jobs in the big city of Johannesburg.

For the original Welgevalers, all this movement was difficult to understand, but it seems that, with the secure base of Welgeval, the younger generation was emboldened to pursue new ideas in new places. After all, they could always return to the farm if things did not work out with their ventures.

Stephanus was not exempt from this wave of activity. He got it into his mind to bundle up his family and go and study further at the newly established theology college in Stofberg so that he could become an ordained minister of the Dutch Reformed Church. Now an active proponent of his uncle's ambition for the Moloto clan, he felt obliged to enrol as one of the first students at this new college for African students of the NG Kerk. He wanted to be the first ordained African minister of the church in the Pilanesberg district. His two eldest daughters, Gadifele and Christina, had almost completed their teacher-training course in Moruleng, and so Stephanus felt confident that, with a few cattle sold and his daughters' additional income, he could raise the required fees for college. He'd also heard that the college allotted each student a piece of land to grow vegetables, assuring students of their livelihood. He planned to take along bags of Welgeval's staple maize so that Elisa could grow all the required vegetables. To top it off, there was the additional benefit of free education for his two youngest children, David and Madira.

And so, in 1926, after weighing up his options and assuring Polomane of his eventual return, he resigned from his teaching post on Welgeval and departed for Stofberg.

True to his word, after three years in Stofberg, Stephanus returned to the farm as a qualified minister of the Dutch Reformed Church. But, much to the annoyance of his father, instead of settling down on Welgeval, he was swiftly posted to the parish of Mokgalwaneng.

Polomane had hoped that Stofberg would put an end to his son's absence from the farm. With Jonathan gone and David travelling frequently, Cornelius was the only constant presence, and the old man struggled more than anyone to understand the itinerant nature of the new generation. But Stephanus shared his uncle's fervent desire to spread the word of God, and Mokgalwaneng provided the perfect opportunity to do so. The village was not too far from Moruleng, and his cousin Martha and her late husband had started a mission there a few years earlier.

Martha's husband had been the first evangelist of this parish, but he died soon after their posting, so the village had been without a minister for quite some time when Stephanus arrived. Although the little school that Martha had set up continued to run after she left, there was no replacement for her husband, with the result that Stephanus almost had to start missionary work from scratch.

For his church, he selected a large tree situated more or less in the middle of the village, not too far from his house. In preparation for his first service, he spent the week visiting all of the villagers and inviting them to church on Sunday. He also visited the school to urge the children to bring their parents along. The teachers were fully behind him. Very few of the adults had ever been to church, but most agreed to attend, mainly out of curiosity about this strange meeting. Not only was it called by a man who wasn't a chief, it also included everybody: men, women and children. This was unheard of: only men attended the chief's meetings in the village.

On Sunday the men collected their leather tanning equipment so that they could continue with their work while they listened to what the stranger had to say. This was normal practice at the chief's meetings, as people maintained that one doesn't listen with one's hands. Women, with their grass mats underarm and children in tow, followed their husbands to the meeting.

When everyone was seated, Stephanus stood up to preach the Good News of the Bible. After careful consideration, he had decided to begin with the story of the crucifixion – how Christ had died for our sins on the cross. Thinking that the story would be a good introduction to Christianity, he explained, in great detail, how Christ was tortured and finally nailed to the cross.

The sermon was going well and Stephanus felt he had the audience in his thrall. But when he reached the point at which a soldier goads Jesus with a sponge dipped in vinegar, the congregation began to grow restless.

"How cruel!" a man in the audience exclaimed, interrupting the sermon.

"What had this poor man done to be killed like that?" another asked. "I've never heard of such vicious cruelty in this whole land of Bakgatla."

"Hush, people," Stephanus pleaded. "You are not supposed to interrupt in church!"

"Not interrupt?" a man shouted. "You called us from our homes to tell us about this man who was killed in this terrible way and you don't want us to comment! Why are you telling us this horrible story, especially in front of our wives and children?"

"People, people, just bear with me and listen. You will soon understand why it all happened," Stephanus went on, entreating his audience. "Christ died to save us."

The audience looked back at him, utterly perplexed. This made no sense.

"Save us from what?" a woman asked.

A man at the back stood up and made a visible and audible point of packing up his goods.

"People," the man announced, "I don't want to end up being accused of complicity in the murder this man is talking about. I'm leaving. I don't want my children to listen to this."

Cries of "True! True!" erupted throughout the congregation, and slowly the villagers collected their things and left.

Thus Stephanus's first church service came to an unceremonious end. He'd never experienced this kind of embarrassment in all his teaching life. He asked Elisa to take the children home and, dejected, sat down to review the debacle. He had always considered himself a good teacher, and most people would agree. But this was not school, he reminded himself. People were used to having their say

Land of My Ancestors

in meetings. Perhaps it was unfair to expect them to sit quietly and listen. It was quite strange for them. He decided that his choice of sermon was perhaps also unfortunate. The gore of the crucifixion was too much. It was difficult for people to understand that it was all for a good purpose. Perhaps he should have begun with the birth of the Christ child. Stephanus decided to take a step back and start all over again.

The following Monday he returned to the school to talk to the children, asking them to explain to their parents how church works. He enlisted the teachers' help to conduct house visits and spent the week knocking on doors. After all these preparations, he felt ready for a new beginning on Sunday. However, although the villagers had listened to his explanations and nodded understandingly, only three families returned for a second helping.

Stephanus decided to seek help from the chief, the only recognised authority in the village. The chief was lukewarm about the church. He saw no special benefit in it nor any harm for that matter, as long as it kept out of his affairs. He accepted that it came as a package with the school, which he appreciated, as he believed it taught the children the "white man's secrets". Stephanus pleaded with the chief that he be allowed to take a few of his advisors to attend a church service in Moruleng so that they could get a sense of how a church service is conducted. The chief agreed.

The visit to Moruleng did the trick. Stephanus's church elders got the idea of how a church should run and, more importantly, they saw the enthusiasm for the new way of life among the villagers of Moruleng. Not wanting their children to miss out on any of the benefits, they changed their approach to Christianity. Slowly, with increasing exposure to the church message, more and more villagers were converted.

35

From the beginning Stephanus had fixed a beady eye on his only son, and soon things started moving along in the direction that promised to fulfil his hopes, although now and again the boy tested his resolve. Stephanus crushed any form of waywardness with immediacy; it had to be done, there really was no choice. Unlike his brothers, who had enough boys to spare, Stephanus had only David, and all responsibility rested on the boy's shoulders. Firstly, there was the Levite baton: it had to be passed on. Who else would take it if his own flesh and blood would not? Lead by example, he insisted. Secondly, someone had to take responsibility for all the women in his family. His son had to be man enough for all that.

After Stephanus had completed his ministry course, David stayed behind to complete his Junior Certificate, but he was soon involved in an escapade at school. Stephanus took the chance to make his point once and for all, nipping any mischievousness in the bud.

Alone, in a deliciously unsupervised space, David was tempted to try out all the things he had been forbidden. One morning, he and some of his friends decided to hold their class teacher hostage. Accusing her of meanness and unfairness, they kept her locked in the class all morning until the principal came to rescue her. This was such a serious offence that the school expelled them, and the parents were called in to account for their children's criminal behaviour and remove them from the campus.

Stephanus rushed to the school to plead for clemency. As a newly ordained minister, this was the last thing he'd thought would bring him back to Stofberg.

"What will be achieved by expelling these boys from the school, except to increase the number of miscreants in our land?" Stephanus grovelled. "They deserve no mercy, but this I beg for us as parents."

Such embarrassment Stephanus had never imagined possible, but the principal finally agreed to give the boys a last chance. Stephanus immediately took his son aside and gave him the dressing-down of his life.

But he was not really satisfied. A misdemeanor of this size required harsher punitive measures. David knew that if he had been living on Welgeval, his skin would have borne the brunt of the misdeed. He had escaped with very little punishment, and an unstated debt lingered in the air.

"*Die klein vloek!*" Stephanus swore as he caught the train back to Mokgalwaneng. "He'll pay for this."

Six months after this event, when Stephanus had just completed his second baptismal service, word came from Welgeval that his father had died. The prophecy that Polomane had uttered after Gonin's death had been forgotten over the years, but Stephanus remembered it now as he rode to the farm. Polomane had followed Gonin to the grave.

He found his stepmother in a state of shock. Her husband's death had been completely unexpected. Maria, now twice-widowed, said that he'd been fine as fettle the day before, weeding the yard and working in the vegetable garden as usual. He went to bed with no complaint of any ailment, and then simply never woke up.

No one knew how old he was when he died, but Polomane and Maja always estimated their age on the basis of Gonin's. They reckoned they were a little older than him, but their children thought that the difference couldn't have been more than five years. Gonin, who had died ten years before, had been seventy-three, so Stephanus and Cornelius judged Polomane to have been about eighty-eight years of age. Slipping away so swiftly was in keeping with Polomane's character. He'd always been a quiet man, not given to making a fuss about anything, but the events that had taken place on Welgeval while Stephanus was away in Stofberg and Mokgalwaneng had rendered him almost mute.

It was Polomane's second son's death that had dealt the fatal blow. On one of his numerous sales trips, David picked up what at first seemed like an annoying chest problem. The problem swiftly became a crisis and proceeded to kill him in a number of days. He died alone in the strange town of Krugersdorp with no family at his side. Polomane was just growing accustomed to Jonathan's death when David was taken, and the thought of his son dying in some foreign town proved too much for the old man. It seemed so cruel that his sons should be taken away, especially since he had expected them to look after him in his old age.

After a brief period of mourning, Polomane's pain turned into anger and his behaviour grew increasingly irrational. He decided to fetch everything that his son owned, reasoning that David's children and cattle should make up for his loss. He would take care of them himself, he argued. So, two weeks after David's death, he sent his herd boys to collect David's cattle, and to inform his son's widow, Mmakentshitswe, of his intention to take custody of the grandchildren. Unsurprisingly, the woman did not take kindly to the news.

"The man is crazy," she objected, as she drove the herd boys off. "I can't lose my husband and everything we possessed. I won't allow him!" She put on her shawl and marched over to Polomane's house to talk some sense into him.

Mmakentshitswe found her father-in-law bent over some sweet potato seedlings in his beloved garden.

"What makes you think that I'm going to give you my cattle?" she shouted as soon as he was in earshot. "How in heaven's name do you expect me to feed my family?"

Polomane straightened up. "I will take care of everything," he replied curtly.

"You must be out of your mind!" she yelled. "Do you think I'm going to let you take my children as well? You really are crazy!"

Polomane ignored her as she ranted and raved, continuing with his gardening as though she was invisible.

"Woman, just leave my house," he said finally, pointing towards the gate. "My mind is made up. I'm fetching everything that belonged to my son and there's nothing you can do about it."

"You are a madman!" Mmakentshitswe screamed. "I promise you, you haven't heard the last of this. I'll set the law on you."

Mmakentshitswe appealed to the family for help, but they sided with Polomane, saying that she had insulted him – a case of blood being thicker than water. Of course, the family also knew that once the old man had made up his mind, they stood little chance of changing it.

But Mmakentshitswe was equally stubborn. She saddled a horse and rode to the Native Affairs Commissioner in Pilanesberg to report the case, with her son, William, seated in front of her. Unfortunately, the commissioner ruled in favour of Polomane, stating that according to customary law, a woman does not inherit her husband's estate. Mmakentshitswe was given custody of the children, but Polomane was allowed to take all the cattle.

Beaten and angry, Mmakentshitswe collected her children and a few personal belongings and went back to her own family in Ramatshabalemao.

Polomane never recovered from this crisis. He withdrew from all social contact completely, not even bothering to go to church any more. Once a month the dominees served him Holy Communion at home. He read his Bible in the evenings, and every morning, Monday to Sunday, he rose at sunrise to work alone in his garden, until one spring morning in September, when he simply slept on.

36

STEPHANUS

We made arrangements for Father's funeral, and I asked one of the dominees from Moruleng to come and conduct the service. Cornelius and my cousins tried to persuade me to preside over it, but I declined. Nothing annoys me more than a snivelling speaker on the podium. I must admit though that my feelings on this occasion were nowhere near the wrenching pain I had felt over my brothers' deaths. In fact, I felt blessed to have had a father up to the ripe old age of fifty. It made up for the early loss of my mother.

I may be overstating it a bit, but I always had the distinct impression that Father took over my mother's role when she died. Don't get me wrong, he was a farmer to the core and as strict as they come, but his concern over me bordered on the motherly: "Faan, did you eat?" he would fuss, or "Why are you not wearing something warm in this weather?"

Later, he shifted this concern to my children. I think he decided to make his role complementary to Uncle's, who took it upon himself to shape my professional life. As a result I always returned to Welgeval to recuperate from any professional ravages I might have suffered. I felt very grateful for Father, and so, instead of a homemade coffin, I offered to buy a smart, shiny one from Rustenburg. There was also the decision about where to bury him, always more complicated in the case of second marriages, but Ma Maria agreed that we bury him next to my mother.

And so two graves stood under the old karee tree, which had grown to a monumental size, presiding over them like a sentinel.

The funeral also gave me the opportunity to mete out the punishment I had promised my son. Because he was the youngest of my father's grandchildren and his namesake as well, David had been Polomane's favourite. I decided, after inviting him to the ceremony, not to send anyone to fetch him from the station. David arrived in Rustenburg very early on the day of the funeral and, after waiting for some time for transport to Welgeval, decided to walk all fifty miles to the farm. It was long after sunset when he arrived. The funeral was over and everybody was preparing to go bed. He was so sad to have missed the funeral that I thought he'd never forgive me, but at least the cost of confronting me had been made clear to him. To drive the point home, I then refused him permission to use his horse and cart, even on his return to school, and he had to get a lift on a friend's bicycle. He'd think twice before crossing me again.

Elisa and I spent the following week sorting out Father's possessions. We were unpacking one of his boxes when I discovered a pile of letters from Van Velden, the Gonins' lawyer. Each of them served as a warning that we were falling behind with our payments for the farm. When I'd left Welgeval to go and study in the Free State, I made a loose arrangement with Cornelius and David that they would take over the responsibility of collecting the annual instalment and submitting it to Van Velden. It was four years since any substantial payment had been made. The last letter contained a definite threat of eviction.

I went straight to Cornelius to find out if he knew about the letters.

"Yes," he said casually. "Father mentioned them some time back, but he insisted that you should take responsibility for them. So I never followed it up again."

"But Nelie," I said, "how could you? You knew Father would forget about them as soon as you finished talking."

Eviction, I thought with dread. What would it mean to us? My goodness, I just couldn't wrap my head around that word. Where would we go? What would the church say? I was scared not so much of the fact that we would be homeless, but of the looming scandal that my family had been thrown out of their home because we'd been irresponsible.

"Nelie, how did we come to this? Why were the payments not made and why was I not told?" I quizzed my brother sternly, even forgetting that he was older.

"Listen, Faan," he quipped. "Don't play minister with me. I tried my damnedest while you were away gallivanting in the Free State. For a while the people paid regularly, but they lost interest. Some even turned quite hostile, saying that you must have used all their money for college. They reckoned that after all this time the debt must be fully paid."

"How could they say that without checking the facts?" I said.

"Come now, Faan," Cornelius replied, "you know that's not how our people think. I got tired of following them up; besides, I don't have authority over them that you had as a teacher."

I decided to plead our case with Van Velden and make a request for new terms, taking Elisa and Martha along for reinforcement.

Van Velden was amenable, appreciating our intention to sort out the matter. After examining his notes, he explained to us that on 27th June 1912 we had agreed to buy the farm for the sum of £2 408, and to date, May 1924, we had only paid a total of £1 616. Thus there was an outstanding balance of £792.

But it wasn't a simple matter of paying this outstanding sum. Van Velden gave us three years to pay off the balance, adding that this had to be done at an interest rate of six per cent, backdated from 1st January 1923. A few alarm bells went off in my head. If it had taken us twelve years to pay £1 616, how could we possibly pay off £792 in three, including interest? I tried to talk him into removing the interest, as it was not part of the original deal, but he wasn't prepared to budge.

"You've already exceeded the original terms of the agreement by far too much," he announced. "There can be no more special conditions."

We thanked him and set off on our mule cart, riding in silence for most of the journey. I couldn't decide whether our trip had been a success or not. I was also trying to formulate what I would tell the people back home. This added interest was a real complication. How would I convince my people to start paying even more when they had already convinced themselves that they had paid off the debt?

Elisa, who knows the nuances of my silences well, left me to simmer in my thoughts without interference. When she felt that the moment was safe, she touched my shoulder gently.

"I think that Van Velden's a really good man, letting us continue to stay on our farm like that," she said. "I'm sure the people will be very happy to hear that we have nothing more to worry about if we pay the outstanding amount."

I ignored her. I knew what she was trying to do: pry me off my worries with a sop. I continued to work out how we would meet these new demands.

"You do agree with me, cousin?" she said to Martha.

Elisa's strategy in such situations was very predictable: she was enlisting Martha's help so that I would be completely outvoted. Even though this was the exact reason I had taken the women along, I was annoyed by the overt workings of their manipulation.

"I do, I do," Martha replied. "Can you imagine what a mess we would be in if the man hadn't heeded our plea? We are really lucky.

I'm sure people will jump at this second chance we have been offered, don't you think so, cousin Faan?"

I still did not say anything, but it was starting to make sense.

Dark blobs of cloud were beginning to gather in the western sky. An unseasonable winter rain was lurking on the horizon. I decided to make this the subject of conversation to lead me out of my corner. Over the years with Elisa, I had learnt that an oblique admission of folly was the best policy. I could never bear the glint of satisfaction in her eyes whenever I came out directly to say that I was wrong.

So, after a good roundabout on the topic of unusual weather, I returned to Van Velden and how to avoid eviction.

"It's a really good thing that we have a chance to redeem ourselves," I said casually. "I would never have forgiven myself if we had been thrown out."

"Indeed, cousin, indeed," Martha nodded.

"I will arrange that I take the church service on Sunday, and I'll use that opportunity to make the announcement. Thank goodness for this successful ending," I said, with a good amount of relief.

They did not catch me watching them, but from the corner of my eye I saw Elisa and Martha pinching each other just as I had finished talking.

Women, so predictable, I thought, as I jerked the reigns and called the mules to move faster.

Church services held by a fully ordained minister were always more formal and serious. Often they were also accompanied by Holy Communion. For the occasion, women dressed in their mother's union uniforms. Missionaries organised local women into prayer groups called "mother's unions", and they designed black and white uniforms, especially for the women, with long sleeves and round collars that showed very little of the body. The uniforms were for special church occasions and were meant to ensure that they all looked "decent".

Everyone else on the farm put on their Sunday best, which unfortunately did not always live up to its name. Some of the men wore ill-fitting jackets that their fathers got from former employers, and, although they were an improvement, hiding the threadbare backs of their shirts, they were hardly smart. But no one paid much attention to what the men wore. The pride the women took in their uniforms more than made up for all the chafed collars and torn shirts.

Nagmaal Sundays stood out from all other Sundays, elbowing out routine for excitement. The old women of Welgeval slipped into their black skirts and tops with glee, forgetting all about their rickety hips as they buttoned up their white collars to complete the uniform.

Crow-like figures then trickled down the slopes of the valley, announcing a holy occasion on the farm. It was always my special pride to preach on Welgeval once in a while.

Elisa and I arrived at the church good and early so we could greet the congregation as they filed in. Children jumped out of the way as their parents walked in. To start the service, Elisa led the mother's union in a hymn, for which they rose, belting it out with uncommon gusto. In these uniforms the mothers acquired hot religious fervour, which was very inspiring to a preacher.

I came in through the side door with the church elders, feeling quite pumped up by the general atmosphere and the good news I was about to announce. My brother Cornelius and brother-in-law Ryk Kerneels sat directly opposite the podium in the front seats. I knew they were anxious to hear what I had achieved, but I thought I shouldn't relieve them too soon. I'd tell them only at the end of the service so that they would appreciate my efforts a little more.

I adjusted my collar and gown and took up my favourite subject, God's Love, preaching to my heart's satisfaction. To conclude the service, and in preparation for the announcement, I expounded on God's promise to watch over us eternally.

"Beloved congregation," I began, lowering my voice to indicate the change in subject. "We've just learnt of God's promise never to leave or forsake us. Indeed, He never does, even though we sometimes push Him away by our deeds ..."

Several members of the congregation hung their heads in shame, no doubt considering their personal shortcomings and praying for forgiveness. My words were having the desired effect.

"Though we failed to make our payments to Van Velden regularly, yet ... yet He is forever faithful," I continued.

All eyes were back on the pulpit.

"This we proved yesterday when we went to make our petition to Van Velden. He agreed to give us a second chance and let us continue staying on the farm, on one condition, and one condition only ..."

"And what's that?" Ryk Kerneels shouted from the front row.

"That we will commit ourselves to making larger payments regularly. We now have a much shorter time to finish paying off our debt."

"*Wag 'n bietjie.*" Ryk Kerneels stood up to interrupt me, forgetting that he was addressing a minister. "Even a Friesland cow stops giving off milk at some time. When is this Van Velden going to stop milking us? When we are dead? In fact, a number of the people who started with these payments are already dead – your father, for example. Doesn't that tell you that this has gone on for too long? What's going on, *ou* Faan?"

I was dumbfounded by this attack and hesitated to find an appropriate response.

"Listen, *swaer*," I explained. "Van Velden said very clearly that we have a balance of £792 and that he was going to add six per cent interest because we exceeded our agreed time. Furthermore he said we have only three years in which to finish paying it off. The big problem is that not all of us have been regular in our payments, you know that …"

"Speak for yourself," Kerneels retorted.

Petrus, my other brother-in-law, then shouted from the back, "I smell a rat. Somebody tell me, is there a middleman here trying to make a pretty penny for himself? Tell me!"

The congregation began to mutter and shuffle. A man at the back stood up and pointed at me.

"Yes, we know some people have had a lot of expenses recently, going to college and so forth!" he yelled. "Where did they get the money for all that?"

Cries of "yes" and "indeed" echoed from the women's side.

In a flash the holiness of the church was forgotten, and I was transformed from Stephanus, the pride of Welgeval, into a cheating, lying scoundrel. I couldn't believe it. I stood there, transfixed, clutching at the podium while competing voices almost tore the roof off, some trying to defend me and others baying for my blood. I shut my eyes and prayed for calm.

Ryk Kerneels then stood up and came forward to the collection table. He struck it repeatedly with his Bible until the shouts were reduced to murmurs.

"*Mense!*" he shouted. "This is the kind of behaviour that Christ sorted out with a whip. I'm sorry I left mine at home."

The murmuring dissolved and all eyes fixed on Kerneels.

"I questioned Van Velden's motives, not my brother-in-law's," he continued. "You should all be ashamed of the things you have said about our brother here. We shall pay as Van Velden wants, and anyone who's not prepared to do so should pack up and go. Finish and *klaar*."

"*Hoor! Hoor!*" the men shouted, making a dramatic u-turn.

The leader of the mother's union then led the congregation out with a hymn about keeping our eyes focused on Jesus.

Two of the church elders dug out my fingers from the pulpit and led me outside into the daylight.

37

By the 1920s, the nine men and four women who had settled on Welgeval in 1864 had multiplied into almost one hundred families, with Polomane's making up the majority. Maja's family was firmly settled in Moruleng, but it was smaller because he had only one son and two daughters. As a result the Moloto surname in the Pilanesberg district was propagated mainly by Polomane's sons. With hindsight, Maja's decision to force his brother-in-law to take on his surname proved to have been prophetic. His theory about the two types of Bakone, namely the Levites and the people of the soil, was now clearly evident among the third generation of Welgevalers, although none of them were ever completely disconnected from the land.

Whereas Stephanus and his cousin Martha were the first among the second generation of Welgevalers to pursue education as a career, the third generation took it as a matter of course and a way of life. It was accepted that the children of Welgeval would complete at least the four years of primary schooling on Welgeval before they could take up adult occupations. The pursuit of further education was a matter of choice, capacity and the availability of funds.

Over time, an itinerant teaching and preaching corps of Welgevalers developed. Spread out in the villages all around Pilanesberg and sometimes much further, they spent most of their time in the places where they worked. This group frequently migrated with their families so that not many of their children went to school on the farm. However, they came home periodically to plough or tend their cattle, supplementing their low salaries with part-time farming.

With the growth of cities such as Johannesburg and Pretoria, a third group of migrants emerged from Welgeval. Young men and women discovered that they could make more money working as domestic servants and labourers in the cities. Welgeval now became a serious exporter of people, who replaced, to a large extent, the laden wagons that used to go off to trade the farm's produce. A few committed young farmers remained, but, as time went on, leaving Welgeval after primary school for a working stint in the city became a rite of passage. Gradually the farm became a place for the very young, the old and the infirm.

Like the soft relentless January rains of the bushveld, the new lifestyle slowly leached out commitment to the farm, and Welgeval began to show the signs of a woman past her prime. Her productivity became erratic. Too many people had sucked at her limp breasts. With the growing number of cattle, which migrant farmers came to depend on, the burden grew too much for her to bear. And yet the more her fecundity declined, the more the youth left to find work in the cities so that they could buy more cattle. Welgeval was caught in a vicious cycle of abuse.

As most of the older generation, who had lived in gratitude to Welgeval, died, the migrants became more and more preoccupied with their new lives, failing to notice the annual instalments trickling down to nothing. A letter from Van Velden cancelling the purchase contract and announcing forfeiture of all the monies paid was a rude awakening. Stephanus had seen it coming, but following his previous experience he feared to mention the looming problem to anyone. He rushed from Mokgalwaneng to Welgeval to persuade Ryk Kerneels and his brothers to rustle together a few animals to sell. He wrote to Van Velden to inform him of their plan, but

Van Velden stopped them in their tracks, saying that he'd had enough of their dysfunctional contract. On top of this, it was winter and their animals were in no shape to fetch the required sum at auction. Van Velden told them that he wanted to sort the matter out finally before all the original buyers were dead and gone. He asked Stephanus to call the people of Welgeval to a final sequestration meeting.

Stephanus was now approaching his retirement years and had already built himself a house on the farm. He was spending more and more time there in preparation for the end of his career. Van Velden's decision not to cooperate was more than a threat to his future – it bore the hallmarks of a devastating tornado. By 1924, they had paid only £123.60 – most of which serviced interest. This interest was the most divisive issue. The people of Welgeval could not understand how their money simply disappeared without affecting their debt. Even Ryk Kerneels was starting to grow suspicious of his brother-in-law.

"After so many years, Faan, do you want to tell me we still haven't finished paying off the farm?" he asked when Stephanus reported their new predicament.

Once more Stephanus tried to plead with Van Velden to give them one last chance, but the man would not hear of it. He gave them an ultimatum: "Pay the entire balance of £998.6.7 within a week, or leave so that I can find a more reliable buyer."

Van Velden knew that the Welgevalers could not put down the balance as he requested. In effect he was giving them an eviction order. There was no doubt that he meant it: in spite of several pleas, he would not even agree to meet with Stephanus.

38

STEPHANUS

I couldn't imagine myself or any of the people of Welgeval agreeing to settle in any of the surrounding villages, even though I'd spent a lot of my youth in Moruleng. My stay there had been purposeful, with an end in sight, and so my spirit never got too attached to the village. Uncle, on the other hand, was now well settled in Moruleng, particularly since his daughter Martha had married the chief. But then he had always had royalty encrypted in his heart. He could find his way to the top of any heap.

In all sorts of ways, the people of Welgeval stood out distinctly, and the ordinary villager looked on them as slightly strange. All our bread-baking, sweet-potato and maize-growing ways were quite different from the villagers' practice of growing sorghum and black-eyed beans. As a group, we would definitely transplant badly. Our language was a mosaic of Afrikaans and Setswana – more densely mottled with Afrikaans among the older generation. Because of increasing intermarriage with the women from the villages, our ways were gradually changing, but in general we remained unreformed outsiders. At the chief's meetings in the village, any Welgevaler could always be seen – slightly separate from the rest of the group – seated alone next to his horse or cart.

The villagers had learnt to read our moods very well: "Watch out, as soon as you hear them calling each other *neef*," they warned. Then sparks would fly, or the Welgevalers would march off in a huff.

The idea of finding an alternative place in the villages was therefore completely inconceivable, so I decided to find a way to deal with Van Velden. But how, I couldn't say. The man wouldn't even see me. I spent days agonising over the matter, rummaging in every corner of my mind for a solution to the problem. Then I decided to enlist the help of Martha and her husband, Chief Ramono. Perhaps he could take over the matter and handle it himself. A man of his authority might be able to deal with the irascible Welgevalers' reactions, and at the same time find a reasonable solution that suited both Van Velden and the community. Chief Ramono also had a vested interest in the problem, as he had been one of the original buyers.

The chief agreed to come to Welgeval on Sunday to address the community after the church service. Sundays were always the best days for meetings that dealt with unannounced topics for discussion. I trusted that because of the chief's attendance the key people would adopt their "Sunday best" manners.

My idea was a great success: not only did the whole community attend the service, but the chief's reputation also held some sway with Van Velden, who agreed to attend at his invitation.

Because I needed to reserve my strength and gather courage to manage responses to the announcement, I left the church proceedings to the elder who had been assigned the service for that Sunday. But when *ou* Stemmer saw the chief and me sitting in the front row, he immediately tip-toed over.

"*Neef*, I can't preach when both you and the chief are here," he whispered in my ear. "It's totally against the church rules. No *ouderling* should preach when a dominee is present."

"Go on, *neef*," I replied, "pretend I'm dead and it's my funeral service."

The women noticed the preacher's discomfort and chanted a

hymn to dilute the tension. I stayed put and waited for Stemmer to start the sermon.

Ou Stemmer took some time to find a verse that would be suitable for the occasion. The women's hymns yielded the necessary spirit to aid him. Finally, he made his way through the sermon, rising to an evangelical flourish that left us feeling blessed. I stood up to give the benediction and called on Chief Ramono to address the people. He took his position at the front of the church as the congregation sat to attention.

"Greetings, my people," the chief started. "I can't say that this is a happy visit. A black cloud hangs over Welgeval."

A stunned silence descended on the church as the chief explained the contents of Van Velden's letter.

"The sad thing is," he continued, "unless we can raise the full outstanding amount now, we will lose not only the farm, but also the monies we've paid so far."

Nelie jumped up immediately: "*Oor my dooie liggaam!*" he shouted. "I tell you, I will not sit and watch a man rob me in broad daylight!"

Ryk Kerneels joined in with his sons: "That will be the day!" they roared.

Just as before, complete pandemonium broke loose, with everybody hurling abuse at Van Velden and me alternately.

One of the chief's advisors, a big burly man, finally stood up and put an end to the uproar: "*Tsie lala*! Hush, you people," he yelled. "You don't carry on like that in front of my chief."

That shut them up immediately.

The chief resumed his announcement: "*Digang makgwafo bagaetsho.* Calm down," he said, unperturbed. "I'm sure we can find a way out of this predicament." He understood his testy relatives and dealt with their outcries with enviable authority and grace.

"I will ask my tribe Bakgatla to come to our rescue and pay off the balance," he continued.

The congregation fell silent again as they considered this possibility.

Van Velden, who had kept a low profile throughout the proceedings, then stood up: "Erm," he grunted, looking as if he expected to be shot, "whoever pays off the balance will get the title deed and ownership of the farm. That's the law."

More commotion erupted.

"What about our money?" the men rumbled.

But in spite of these protests the chief and Van Velden prepared to leave, and, realising that there was nothing more to be done, the congregation filed out of the church. Through-out the afternoon disgruntled expressions of disapproval and worry erupted in households all over Welgeval.

Two weeks later, Chief Ramono returned with both good and bad news: the tribe had agreed to pay the balance, but they were not prepared to refund us anything. They said that we either accept the deal or they withdraw their offer. With our backs up against the wall, we agreed to take it. The chief, however, assured us that while the tribe would take ownership of the farm, we would, in recognition of the amounts we'd paid, be allowed permanent residence there.

"I'm sure we trust each other enough to find this a satisfactory solution," he concluded.

No one responded.

Realising that we had escaped the worst outcome, I dared to stand up to show appreciation for the offer. I also thought that the chief was being fair. I was just grateful for the lifeline that he had thrown us.

"Thank you, sir, for your kind assistance," I said. "I'm sure every one of my brothers here agrees that you've saved us from a very difficult situation ..."

"Speak for yourself, Faan, speak for yourself," Nelie interrupted. "I know how much I've paid for this land. Let that man divide it and give us the portion we have paid for."

I couldn't believe my ears. I had worked so hard to secure this deal and again the community threw it back in my face.

"I agree with Cornelius, Chief," Kerneels quipped. "We can't just throw our money into a bottomless pit. Let's divide the farm according to the amounts we've paid. Bakgatla can then buy what is left over."

The chief nodded understandingly. "We shall see," he replied. "I don't know if it can be done like that. We'll have to discuss it with Van Velden."

I stood up and prayed to conclude the proceedings, and the congregation filed out, much more muted than usual.

I took a few weeks' leave from work and stayed on Welgeval to finish up sorting out our problem. I also needed to put the finishing touches to my house, which I was readying for my retirement at the end of the year. I went to bed unusually early that Sunday evening.

My people's reaction to the whole ordeal hurt me very much. How could they turn against me like that? With hindsight I realised that I was better acquainted with the Bakgatla, so I saw no threat in letting them have the title deed of the farm, but, at the time, I felt greatly aggrieved.

One evening, shortly after the second meeting, I woke up with a splitting headache in the small hours of the morning. I sat up and held my head in my hands, groaning.

"What's wrong, Father?" Elisa asked worriedly.

"I have this horrible headache. It's driving me mad."

"I'll put on the light and see if I can find you some tablets," she said, springing into action.

"No light, please, I couldn't bear it."

Elisa fetched her medicine box and rummaged through it in the moonlight. There were no tablets. She picked a small root of *serokolo* and gave it to me to chew. I bit into the wretched thing and swallowed the bitter juice, hoping for immediate relief, but it took much longer than I'd hoped. After about an hour I dozed off again.

I woke at my usual time of five o'clock in the morning. The room was already light, bathed in the glow of the impending sunrise. I was shocked to see green stripes painted over everything in the room: our clothes hanging over the chair, our blankets – everything in the room had broad green stripes running down them. I got up and looked through the window and there were the same stripes everywhere, even on the trees.

"Elisa, Elisa, what have you done?" I moaned, covering my eyes with my hands. "What are all these stripes about?"

"What stripes?" she replied. "What are you talking about?"

"This," I said, running my hand down one long stripe that ran down the blanket. "What is this?"

Elisa gave me a perplexed look: "Your headache must be very bad," she said. "Please go back to sleep, Pa."

"I'm not sick," I said as I crawled under the blankets, feeling dizzy from all the stripes. "I just want to know."

Suddenly the whole room went very dark, and I was more scared than I had ever been in my life. I lay there, thinking the end had come, while a great weariness overtook me. I'm not sure how long I lived in that darkness, but Elisa says I was ill for two weeks. She tells me they had to fetch a healer from Moruleng, who boiled up various roots for me. I remember none of this. I really don't

Land of My Ancestors

know what happened, but it seems that my body just gave in to all the anxiety and worry about Welgeval.

Once I had regained my health, I was told that Chief Ramono had managed to raise the required amount of money and was waiting for me to get well so that we could take it to Van Velden. When I was fully recovered, he called Van Velden to come and collect the money the Bakgatla had raised. The chief had successfully mobilised each family to contribute five shillings to make up the sum of £1 000, including transfer costs. By this time, four of the original nine purchasers had died, but their heirs and the five remaining buyers were asked to sign a pledge forgoing all the money they had paid towards the purchase of the farm; £1 600 was signed away in the process.

Nelie and Ryk Kerneels stood fast to their earlier decision not to sign such an agreement. They insisted on having portions equivalent to the amounts they had paid cut out to them, and Van Velden agreed to investigate this possibility. After consultation with the Commissioner of Native Affairs, he came back with the news that they could only take ownership if they had their portions surveyed and cut at their own expense. But they couldn't afford to do this, so they lost their land along with the rest of us.

In May 1933, ownership of the farm Welgeval was transferred to the tribe of Bakgatla.

39

STEPHANUS

The day of my departure from Mokgalwaneng finally arrived after a month of intense activity, sorting out documents, and making sure everything was up to date and ready for the handover to the new minister. Elisa and her mother's union spent the time scurrying about like a bunch of hens, organising the farewell function for Sunday. It was a good occasion. All the dominees from the main mission in Moruleng were there, including one or two from Pretoria. The mother's union and the youth choirs sang their hearts out, praising the Lord with everything they had. A lump rose in my throat as I looked back to the beginning and realised just how far I'd come with my congregation. After twenty years, we had a vibrant church that could stand its ground next to any in the district. I was sad to leave, but I also felt that I'd had my innings and deserved the rest, or perhaps just a change in lifestyle.

So much had changed since the missionary work started in Pilanesberg. Our mission church was now dissociated from the Cape Synod and affiliated with the Pretoria Central Synod. There were a few more of us who were fully ordained. We were proud of our achievements, but, despite the fact that we received similar training, the church never really accorded us equal status with our white counterparts. Our salaries were a sore point and remained the main means of discriminating African from white ministers. The church's racial policies were also expressed in the paternalistic allocation of authority. It would not allow a white man to work under an African regardless of his qualifications and experience, but a white minister was always expected to oversee an African minister or evangelist.

A young nephew of mine, Saki, Nelie's son, had a serious run-in with this kind of attitude. After establishing a vibrant church for the workers on a tobacco farm in the Brits district, the Central Synod in its wisdom decided to send a white dominee to form a church for the white farmers and also oversee Saki's work. This meant that Saki's congregation would not only have to bear the costs of their own church, but would also have to contribute to the running of the white church. Much like his father, my nephew was not the type to take such things lying down. He complained to the Synod about this exploitation of poor people and threatened to break away from the church. The church wouldn't budge from its position, and so, with his congregation right behind him, Saki broke away from the Dutch Reformed Church and formed his own church, which he called the Bantu Reformed Church.

As I packed my wagon to leave Mokgalwaneng for good, I was happy to leave all the struggles with the Church Synod to younger men.

I was confident that, despite all the squabbles over our negotiations to continue living on Welgeval, we would eventually heal all the rifts. There was still some simmering bitterness among us, and from time to time I also battled with a feeling of guilt about the whole thing. All our quarrels about payments and the final loss of the farm filled me with shame. I wondered if I could have done more to ensure regular payments. Should I ever have left to go and study in Stofberg? Did I let the farm go too easily? Should I have taken a bolder stand, like Nelie and Kerneels, and demanded that they cut us portions of the farm according to the amounts we had paid? But where would we have found the money to pay for all the surveys they required? I strongly believe that we came out with the best solution, given the nightmare of eviction that we faced. I suppose the case will be left for history to judge. I decided not to spend my life stewing in guilt.

But this was easier said than done, because, for the first few weeks after our arrival on Welgeval, my feelings swung back and forth between hope and guilt. I found it difficult to face my daily life and the glum faces of my brothers and cousins. Fortunately, the business of settling down soon left me with no energy to nurse these unstable emotions. Elisa and I decided to add a kitchen and an extra room to the house we had already built. She was no longer happy to cook in the *buitekamer* as she did when we visited, and insisted that we have enough space for our children and grandchildren when they came to stay.

Shortly after my arrival at Welgeval, my eldest daughter, Gadifele, who had stayed behind to teach in Mokgalwaneng, suffered a devastating blow: a few days before she was due to marry, her fiancé died. After his death, she left teaching and took up a job as a housekeeper in Johannesburg. I can't say I was happy with this, but we went along with her decision, only because we hoped it would give her a chance to start a new life. Christina, my second, married a minister of the Dutch Reformed Church like myself and settled in Potchefstroom, while Madira, my youngest, will soon complete her midwifery course in Johannesburg. A young man from Pietersburg is waiting in the wings to marry her.

But I'm particularly pleased about what my son David has achieved. In spite of the initial hiccups and the debacle with my father's funeral, he has exceeded my expectations by a long measure.

After finishing his Junior Certificate examinations, my son immediately agreed to take up a position at Bethesda College, a newly opened college of the NG Kerk in the northern Transvaal, where he would work and save up for further studies. It was now plain to see that he was determined to follow a life of education. After three years, he had saved enough money to study for matric. He enrolled at Lovedale College, my alma mater, to complete his Matric Certificate. Because of limited funds, David and his friends, already in their late twenties, organised study shifts, swotting into the wee hours of the mornings, keeping awake by wrapping wet towels around their heads. They condensed the two-year programme and passed matriculation in just one year.

I was not only thrilled by the news that David had passed matric, but amazed at how God answers even the most casual prayers. I remembered my vow when I abandoned my studies to marry Elisa.

"Matric! ... what did I tell you?" I enthused with my wife. "Didn't I say I'd give you a son?"

Looking over my life like this makes me happy about all that I have. I'm truly grateful for the nurturing from Welgeval. With every passing day I find new things for which I can thank her. One of these is my vegetable garden, which I planted along the river soon after we arrived. It yields a wonderful crop. As I loaded my first wagon-load of sweet potatoes and other vegetables to sell, I found myself falling in love with Welgeval all over again, only my affection was private and furtive, unlike the wild and open love affair of my father's. Yet I'm completely energised by it. Each stroke of my plough is a caress to which Welgeval responds most generously. But I'd be lying if I said that ownership of the farm no longer matters, yet the pleasure of being here and the certainty of one day lying next to my parents' graves is enough to keep me happy.

I must have strained my heart with all these different types of emotions, because when I went to see the doctor about the chest pain I'd had since our return, he advised me to take it easy and look after myself. I thought I had pulled a muscle while working in the fields, but he said I had a bad heart and should avoid strenuous work. I was taken aback, especially by the advice.

"How can you live on Welgeval without doing strenuous work?" I scoffed. "My father worked strenuously until his last day. These modern doctors!"

I continued with my normal routine, but as time went by I found it more and more difficult to cope with my work, as I tired very easily and had to stop to catch my breath every few minutes.

It came to a point where I could no longer defy the doctor, and now faced the possibility of spending the rest of my life sitting on the stoep waiting for death. Impossible! Death, I decided, would have to catch up with me. I had things to do.

I sold a few cattle and built myself a little store in order to supply the people of Welgeval with their groceries. This was to be my "less strenuous" work for the rest my life. I was very happy with it, and so were the people.

Unfortunately, the church authorities were not. They never approached me directly, but now and again I heard of their displeasure with my trading occupation. Some went so far as to suggest that I was a disgrace to the church for doing something that was totally inappropriate for a man of the cloth. I heard but did not listen. What did these people think? I had received a meagre once-off pension when I retired. What did they expect me to live on?

I went right ahead and derived enormous pleasure from my new life. I made arrangements to take driving lessons with my friend Stuart, a Scotsman who had married a woman from Moruleng. He was a motor mechanic and sold used cars. When I needed a van to ferry goods from Rustenburg to Welgeval and Stuart did not have one, we decided to convert one of his blue Ford sedans into a van. Two months later I drove my own spanking blue Ford bakkie home, and that was something! The hills of Welgeval echoed with the women's ululation as they came out to witness my little motor, roaring noisily and shattering the silence of the Pilanesberg valley. I don't think I ever felt happier over anything, and from that day I always found an excuse to tear through the dusty roads and exercise my right as the first motorist of Welgeval. I hear that the church authorities' displeasure grew by a decibel. My nephew Saki came to report to me, in a rather distressed state, that he had mentioned my ill-health to them with less than favourable results.

"Who's Reverend Moloto?" they quipped sourly. "Do you mean the businessman?"

I assured him that such reactions are to be expected. With the salaries we had earned, we were obviously not meant to afford luxuries such as cars. But, if truth be told, I was much too excited about my little jalopy to let their concerns bother me. I was able to deliver groceries further afield instead of jogging around on the old donkey cart. I often loaded my grandchildren into the van and we set off on the bumpy roads. Nobody's displeasure could ever take away from the joy we felt on those rides.

40

The University of Fort Hare stood just across the road from Lovedale College, and David and his friends enviously watched the few young men who walked in and out of the hallowed gates of the university. Now armed with a Matric Certificate, the entry requirement to university, David wasted no time in making the necessary arrangements to gain admission. His father stood ready and willing to sell any number of cattle to see his son through his momentous studies.

David, the first from Welgeval to study at this dizzying level, felt obliged not only to achieve the degree, but also to soak up and take home as much of the university aura as possible.

Then Fort Hare was also geared to distinguish its students from the run-of-the-mill African. Based on the aims of British tertiary education, its intention to produce "gentlemen" was clearly stated. David and his colleagues did not disappoint.

They adopted the ways of the gentleman, from the sublime to the ridiculous. For instance, the boys embraced a productive work ethic, but also acquired the art of cigarette-smoking. They dressed like gentlemen and took up English as their lingua franca. Overall, they grew to fit the bill, but every now and then a slip would chip off the gentleman's veneer, revealing their real background.

One day David walked into a shop to buy his first waistcoat, a standard item for the gentleman of the time. After browsing for ten minutes, he asked the shop assistant for a petticoat, thinking that this was the name for the small coat he wanted. Welgeval lay not too far from the surface.

Towards the end of his studies, David decided to round off his gentleman's image by differentiating himself from the many David Polomanes of Welgeval who had been named after his grandfather. He "poshed up" his names, changing David to Davidson after his English professor and role model at Fort Hare, Davidson Don Jabavu; he then anglicised Polomane to Pelman. When he completed his degree, he wrote to inform his father of these gentlemanly changes, introducing himself as Davidson Pelman Moloto. Stephanus agreed that the new names suited a university graduate.

It took a long time for Stephanus to get used to such achievement in his family. It outstripped by far what he had expected in answer to his prayer for his son to do better than him, almost making up for the loss of Welgeval. His cup was filled to the brim.

"From Welgeval to Fort Hare ... a graduate in the family ... who would ever have thought ...?" he muttered repeatedly to his equally proud wife.

Typical of the third generation of Welgevalers, who having lived in other parts of the country felt the pull of Welgeval much less, Davidson decided to take up a teaching post at Wilberforce College. This was a teacher-training college run by black American missionaries of the African Methodist Episcopal Church (AME) at a township called Evaton, just outside Johannesburg. It offered an interesting curriculum, made more vibrant by its emphasis on the arts, especially music. The church services swayed to Negro spiritual choruses, a far cry from the dowdy hymns of the Dutch Reformed Church. Davidson took to Wilberforce like a fish to newly discovered pond water. He met many dynamic students at college, and in no time at all he had also spotted a pretty young woman in the choir, whom he was determined to take as his wife.

The object of his desire was one Khwiti Letanke, who was doing a teacher's course at the college. Khwiti grew up in the village of

Mabaalstad, also in the western Transvaal, where she stayed with her aunts while her mother, Paulina, worked as a domestic servant in Johannesburg. Paulina had married Daniel Letanke, an ANC stalwart and journalist of the newspaper *The Bantu World*, but the match ended in divorce. Still, Paulina was determined to give her two daughters the life she had never had. She was proud to have worked her way up the ranks of the Johannesburg domestic workers and into the households of the richest white families, who were able to pass on pretty hand-me-downs to her daughters. She managed to save up enough money to pay for their college education, while also supporting her family in Mabaalstad.

"I really hope you'll finish college and be a teacher, so you don't scrub floors like me," Paulina would often say.

With all the cast-off clothes from her mother's well-to-do madam, Khwiti was always well turned out, and she sang beautiful solos in the college choir. This combination formed a heady mix for the young man from Welgeval, and soon he wrote to his father to inform him of his intention to marry. He even bought a plot of land in Evaton on which he hoped to build a house for his family.

Stephanus wrote back, after making sure that Khwiti was not a total stranger from the city, and gave the union his blessing. But, like his father before him, he also expressed concern about Davidson's decision to settle so far away.

"*A o latlha go lebaleba,*" he complained. "Are you really going to bury us alive like that?"

This tugged at Davidson's conscience, so he applied for a principal's post at the newly established secondary school at Phokeng, not too far away from Welgeval, where he knew many obligations awaited him.

41

It is implicit in the unwritten code of conduct for a gentleman's wife that she should never work outside the home. But was it really meant to apply to a young bride who had just moved to a new village where most of the women of her age had gone to work as domestic workers in Johannesburg? There were two primary schools in the village of Phokeng, and Khwiti would have given anything to take up a post at Phokeng Preparatory School. That it was also run by black American missionaries of the Episcopalian church fuelled her frustration because she felt that, through teaching at the school, she could relive her treasured experience of Wilberforce and reduce her yearning for life in the city.

But a working wife was not part of Davidson's plans. He lived by the creed that a gentleman's wife supports him in his career, and he in turn takes care of all her needs.

So many times Khwiti appealed to her husband to let her go and teach, especially when they enrolled their eldest daughter at the school.

"Really, my dear," Khwiti would implore, "don't you think I would be better able to monitor Kidi's education if I was teaching at the school?"

"And what would happen when we have other children?" was Davidson's standard response.

They both wanted a big family, and so she could not argue with him. Khwiti grew weary of and frustrated by this brick wall. She felt that all her hard-earned education had come to naught. In her mind she had also been robbed of an opportunity to fulfil her promise to her mother – that she could retire as soon as she started working. But Davidson stressed that he was man enough to look after all the women in his own family, his mother-in-law included.

The sad irony was that when Davidson and Khwiti did have children, they had four daughters and one son, and unashamedly Davidson encouraged his daughters to study as far as they could, even setting the acquisition of a profession as a condition they should satisfy before they could get married. That, he said, was to ensure that they would be self-supporting even in marriage. The double standard galled Khwiti.

"I wonder what I could have done if I'd been given a chance," she would sometimes fume when Davidson crowed about one of his daughter's achievements.

"They couldn't have done it without you, my dear," he would retort, quite puzzled by his wife's attitude.

"That's what you think," she'd huff. "What about my life ..."

Davidson was quite perplexed by this anger and dissatisfaction. He thought a woman would be happy to have a responsible man. But no number of "nice things" he bought could heal the hurt Khwiti felt, especially when she met professional women of her age. She managed to sidetrack her frustration in a newly discovered talent: sewing and dressmaking.

She made beautiful clothes not only for herself and her daughters, but also for women in the community. Young girls in need of wedding dresses and fine apparel soon knocked on her door.

As the days went by, Davidson drew energy from his new senior post in Phokeng, as well as its closeness to Welgeval. A love of the soil still resonated in his heart. But, more practically, he saw a chance to augment his salary with farming. Once a month and during school holidays, he and his family trekked from Phokeng to Welgeval to see to his cattle and plough his mielie fields.

He set out to build his school quickly, recruiting good teachers from different parts of the country, and it thrived. A keen footballer himself, Davidson took charge of the school team, and in no time it was a drawcard for the school. His students came not only from Phokeng, but also from villages further away in the district of Rustenburg.

For many years Bafokeng High School was the only secondary school for Africans in the district of Rustenburg. Davidson's house soon turned into a mini-boarding school. Every year he would bring home one or two outsiders who wanted to study at his school but could not find accommodation in the village. Parents expected as much from a school principal. Why would he run a school if he wouldn't also keep the children, they argued, very often forgetting that there were fees and sundry expenses to be paid, which Davidson and Khwiti had to provide.

Part of the gentleman's training at Fort Hare University involved a continued focus on education. Students were encouraged to remain productive in educational matters throughout their lives. Davidson's anthropology professor, noting the dearth of literature written in African languages, encouraged them to write books and novels in their own languages, and somewhere Davidson found the time to pen and publish his first Setswana novel, *Mokwena*, shortly after the birth of his first daughter, thus becoming the first Setswana novelist. He discovered that writing could also help to supplement his income, and so he went on to write a total of five novels, all planned but not successfully executed, to celebrate the births of his five children.

42

A few years after Davidson had settled in Phokeng, his cousin Ernest took up a principal's post in Moruleng. Ernest had grown up in Ramatshabalemao, where his mother Matshinagwe had settled after her big fight with Polomane. As a result, Ernest and his older brothers, Abram and William, had had a much harder life, without the support of Welgeval. Ernest studied through correspondence to obtain his degree and prove his ability to beat the odds. Davidson and Ernest were the stars of the Welgeval Levites – parents pointed to them as role models to emulate.

But a quiet rivalry developed between the two young Moloto men, with each trying to outdo the other, especially in matters of education. Davidson established himself as a writer, while Ernest continued with his studies, eventually obtaining a doctorate in Setswana from the University of South Africa.

Ernest had two sons, who were a little older than Davidson's children, and so he seemed to have the upper hand both in education and in the child-bearing stakes. He claimed his place in the clan first, naming his youngest son Bakone Justice.

Davidson's only son, on the other hand, was born after two daughters, almost at the point of despair. At the news of his grandson's birth, Stephanus shouted "*Otukile*", which is short for "the fire is kindled", and so the boy was named Otukile Stephanus, after his grandfather. Then Davidson "poshed up" the second name to Stevenson, so that it was in keeping with his own.

By the time Davidson's and Ernest's children went to school in

Land of My Ancestors

the fifties and sixties, provision of secondary education in South Africa had increased remarkably. Missionary education was flourishing, and a number of boarding schools were established throughout the country, of which one of the most famous was Bethel Training College, near the town of Lichtenburg in the western Transvaal. Families scraped together money to send their children to study at such boarding schools. Not only did they offer an opportunity to leave the village and get a better education, but more often than not they were also the only means of getting post-primary education.

Although Ernest's brother Abram did not distinguish himself academically, he was nevertheless the first in the family to send a son to Bethel Training College for secondary education and a teacher's course. This made the boy, Bosman, a trailblazer for the fourth generation of Moloto children.

But Bosman also blazed a trail in another direction. The ANC Youth League was growing, with vibrant young leaders in the newly elected persons of Nelson Mandela and Oliver Tambo. Boarding schools became fertile recruiting grounds for the movement. But the seed for the movement was planted early in Bosman's life. Abram was employed on the railways in Johannesburg and was very active in the labour movement. He used to tell young Bosman about the activities of the ANC, and sometimes he brought his friends from the movement with him when he came home on leave. It was therefore a natural progression for Bosman to join the Youth League at college. After completing his studies, he came back home to teach, and immediately took up political activities in his spare time, forming a branch of the Youth League in Pilanesberg.

In 1960 the apartheid government swooped down on the ANC and procceded to clean up all its cells. Bosman was caught in the net. A shock wave reverberated through the Moloto clan. Davidson and Ernest, in particular, were traumatised.

"How could one of us get arrested? A teacher for that matter!" they clucked and moaned. Around Pilanesberg at the time, the only people who were ever arrested were cattle thieves. Davidson and Ernest had long decided to keep their noses out of politics and stay focused on their education mission.

Bosman was held for three months without trial at the Johannesburg Fort prison. He was suddenly released without explanation, but from then on he was a marked man, sporadically arrested whenever the government conducted raids on the resistance movements. Soon his continued imprisonment took its toll on him. He lost weight and came down with a cough that would not respond to any of the usual medication.

The clan gasped again. Bosman had tuberculosis – a disease they had thought was for miners only! It ate him up, weakened him, and finally he succumbed to it on the third of October 1970. And so the Moloto clan made its first sacrifice to apartheid.

They prayed that it would be the last. Ernest and Davidson were particularly determined to keep their sons out of it.

43

Tormented by the growing resistance to apartheid, Hendrik Verwoerd, then Minister of Native Affairs, borrowed Hitler's approach and devised a final solution that would deal with the root cause of all the troubles: missionary influence on African education. Verwoerd and others believed that missionary education had inculcated unrealistic expectations in Africans and that these needed to be reversed. So, in 1953, the apartheid government implemented the Bantu Education Act in an attempt to wrest all control of education from Africans and secure it firmly in a central ministry of Bantu Education. Bantu Education would provide a special curriculum with the aim of developing a servile class suitable for the manual labour required by the economy.

All missionary schools were shut down, and the ensuing revolt from the African teaching fraternity was swiftly crushed. Some teachers went into exile, not wanting to work in the hated system. But the die was cast for those who remained. The government then set out to create the management infrastructure for the new ministry of Bantu Education. A schools inspectorate was introduced. White men were employed as inspectors of schools, and a subordinate position of supervisor was created for black men to assist them. In keeping with apartheid policy, this grading of posts respected skin colour first and qualifications last.

In December 1956, Davidson was "promoted" and became one of the supervisors overseeing education in the districts of Rustenburg, Swartruggens and Zeerust. Ernest was promoted soon afterwards.

Shortly after his son's promotion, Stephanus's heart condition deteriorated, perhaps out of the sheer strain of dealing with all the happy events that had tumbled down on him in recent times. His children were well settled with their families and had presented him with thirteen grandchildren. Davidson was moving into realms he did not understand, but progress was all he hoped for. He spent his days on the stoep with Elisa, either reading the Bible or trying to project into the future to see all the good things that would come to Welgeval. He hired a young man to help him with the shop and to drive him around in his van on any trips he wished to make.

"I see many people coming here to Welgeval," he would say to Elisa and his children when they came to visit.

"Coming to do what, Father?" they replied.

He wouldn't explain, and only smiled and repeated, "I see people coming."

Stephanus went to bed early one evening after supper, complaining of fatigue. He never woke up. In the morning, when Elisa awoke, she found that he had gone in the same fashion as his father. Heart failure seems to be the chariot that transports the Molotos across to the other life. They never announce their departure, but are always spared the struggle with death.

And so Stephanus escaped the full travesties of the new apartheid system and the systematic devaluation of the education tradition that he and other black South Africans like him had treasured so much.

At about the same time as Stephanus's death, Khwiti's mother finally decided, after years of labouring as a domestic worker, to hang up her apron. Davidson suddenly found that he had to take full responsibility for three households: his mother's in Welgeval, his mother-in-law's in Tlhabane and his own. Nimbly, he packaged his responsibilities to fit in with one another.

He sent his wife and youngest daughter to Welgeval to take

over the running of his father's little shop and keep an eye on his mother's household. He then dispatched his eldest daughter to boarding school, and took the three younger children to go and live with his mother-in-law in Tlhabane township, outside Rustenburg, where he had his office. This way he could check on the children and his mother-in-law on Thursday evenings before he went to the office to write his report. On Friday evenings he would pick them up and they would spend the weekend with Khwiti on Welgeval.

When they finished primary school, all the Moloto children were sent to boarding school for matric. It was Bakone, the son of Ernest, who was the first to attend university. He attempted a Bachelor of Science degree at the newly established University of the North, which the apartheid government had established along tribal lines to cater for Sotho and other non-Nguni groups.

The degree was new in the African university programme, and ambitious parents like the Levites of Welgeval identified it as the new educational frontier for their children to conquer, often forgetting to take account of natural inclination. But passing a BSc at university was as difficult as pushing a camel through the eye of a needle. The lecturers controlled the pass rate on the basis of all sorts of mysterious criteria. They predicted right at the beginning of the year, even before they knew any of the students, the exact number that would get through. And so it wasn't too surprising when Bakone flunked. He abandoned the BSc degree and sought ministerial permission to study law at Fort Hare University, which at the time was reserved solely for Xhosas. Permission was granted only because the degree was not offered at the University of the North.

Law proved to be Bakone's forte. He did well in his studies and distinguished himself as a debater. By the time he had completed his degree, he was heavily involved in student politics, presiding over the University Christian Movement (UCM), which was a multiracial front to fill the vacuum left by the banned ANC and PAC student movements. He travelled to and from different universities, mobilising students and keeping the revolutionary spirit going. But in a few years' time, the UCM, which black students always saw as too tame to achieve their aims, was replaced by a strong black consciousness student movement that espoused black self-reliance. The South African Student Organisation (SASO) was formed, and black student politics took on a radical form once more, which pitted them against the nationalist government.

Otukile followed Bakone to Fort Hare University, and likewise enrolled for a BSc degree. Two years into his studies, he was also deeply entrenched in SASO politics.

For a while Otukile kept his political involvement far from his father's ears, but all that changed when it started affecting his ability to pass exams. Involvement in politics also happened to be one of the criteria that prevented a student from passing. Soon the government started sniffing at their heels, and a bitter conflict with their clean-nosed parents ensued. With Bosman's death still fresh in their memory and the heavy clan investment in the boys' educational success, Davidson and Ernest insisted on education first, politics later. But, for the boys, it was political freedom first and foremost.

The young black consciousness radicals had just discovered Mao Tse Tung, and looked on him as one of their political gurus. Because Mao's *Little Red Book* was banned in the country, knowledge of its contents lent a special mystique to all those who were secretly wired enough to have come across it. They lived and breathed the *Little Red Book*.

One day, in one of the family clashes about keeping out of politics, Otukile let loose his radical inspiration and dared to remind his father that "the chairman never went to school".

"Which chairman?" Davidson thundered.

"Chairman Mao," Otukile replied heroically.

"There is no chairman in my house. If there's to be one, it'll be me!" Davidson blustered, thoroughly annoyed by the idea that he had to run his family life according to the dictates of this little Chinese man.

"And while you are under my care, you will do things as I say!" he added.

But all this insistence on education first proved to be fruitless on the part of Davidson and other fathers who tried to stop the Young Lions. The political tide was too strong, and their sons had jumped in fully clothed. The agenda of the Welgeval Levites was a distant myth to the young men, who were dancing to a louder drumbeat. It was only a matter of time before the Nationalist government clamped down on all student activists, including Bakone and Otukile.

Bakone was placed under house arrest in the small town of Mafikeng, where he had never spent a day in his life. Shortly thereafter, Otukile fled the country, following SASO's rally celebrating Frelimo's independence. He ended up in Botswana, from where he proceeded to live in many different countries, finally spending fourteen years in exile. A little later, Davidson's third daughter also fled to Botswana to marry a young man who was already living in exile, and his youngest daughter was thrown out of university for involvement in SASO activities.

A nasty rumour started doing the rounds in the Pilanesberg district: "A terrible malaise has befallen the Molotos," the people whispered. "Their children have become terrorists! Who would ever have thought?"

44

Against the backdrop of all the student turmoil, the apartheid regime concentrated its efforts not only on repressing these activities, but also on implementing its policy of grand apartheid or separate development, which it believed would solve the native "problem" once and for all. This policy extended the segregation of races by dividing South Africa into a mainly white urban core surrounded by a group of self-governing tribal homelands. The homelands policy of self-governance was offered as a sop to satisfy and stem all African political aspirations.

To give substance to the policy, the government embarked on a vigorous programme of forced removal. This involved uprooting individuals and families referred to as "surplus people" from urban areas and resettling them in the homelands. Villages that were considered to be too close to white areas were also destroyed and moved to the homelands. Mabaalstad, where Khwiti grew up, was one such village. Civil servants were also transferred to homelands to establish the administration infrastructure, often with promotion to posts that they could not, according to the policy of job reservation, occupy in the white areas. For Africans in the homelands, the sky is the limit – so the propaganda for separate development went.

After a short stint as a supervisor in Rustenburg, Davidson was transferred to Lichtenburg, where he worked for two years, and then transferred to Potchefstroom, where he spent a relatively longer time – four years. The family resided in the township of Ikageng, where Khwiti was very happy, as it was the most urban and vibrant of places they'd lived in since they had married. She flourished in her dressmaking, as the township had a larger market. But Davidson returned home from work on New Year's Eve in 1969 with a letter of transfer and a promotion to the post of inspector of schools, based in Welbedacht, a resettlement area in the Zeerust district. He was asked to report for duty on the second of January 1970.

Khwiti was devastated. "Who in their right mind would want to go and live in Zeerust?" she wailed.

But there really was no choice. If Davidson wanted to continue working as a civil servant, they had to go.

The one-street bushveld town of Zeerust, once the resting place of Boer trekkers from the Cape, was quite uninspiring. And the settlement of Welbedacht, situated in an empty valley thirty kilometres west of the town, was a bleak, soul-destroying place. It was made so not only by its isolation, but also by the collection of about a hundred newly built houses, especially designed for unwanted people. The whole complex had been constructed within a few months in three phases. The first phase involved building rows of "toilets in the veld", which the government used to indicate a prospective resettlement area. Next, they built the one-roomed corrugated iron shacks for pensioners and dependants drawn from urban areas and white farms. The shacks were a standard housing provision for all Africans who wouldn't be able to pay rent. The next phase saw the erection of two- and four-roomed brick houses for the employed Africans who would pay monthly rent to the white local representative of Bantu Affairs.

Davidson was allocated a four-roomed house for his family. The house was situated next door to his office, which would form the headquarters of the inspectorate for the circuits of Zeerust and Swartruggens. Viewed from one angle, it could be said that he never had an easier work arrangement. There were no long trips to the office – all it took was a leap over the fence and he could jump back for a hot meal at lunch time – but unfortunately he spent most of his time in the districts. To keep herself busy, Khwiti set up a little shop to provide groceries for the local community.

A further development to the homeland programme kicked in two years later when a self-governing homeland for Setswana-speaking people was established out of the many African villages scattered throughout the western Transvaal, the northern Free State and parts of the Northern Cape. The homeland was called Bophuthatswana (meaning "where Batswana will gather"). All the resettlement areas in the region, including Welbedacht, were added to the homeland, but its borders snaked around the nearby white settlements and towns, leaving them as part of the white core. In line with the tribal design of the homelands, tribal chiefs were sought to lead the homeland administration. In 1972, Lucas Mangope, a tribal chief and former school principal at his village of Motswedi in the Zeerust district, was installed as leader of Bophuthatswana. In partnership with the South African government, a team of consultants was immediately employed to identify a project that would make the homelands viable.

In 1975, five years after arriving at Welbedacht, Davidson reached retirement age, and for the first time in many years he was free to decide on his next move. Does the family stay on in Welbedacht, or do they return to Welgeval? The couple was now tired of setting up home from scratch, and so they chose to stay put in Welbedacht. Davidson decided to become a migrant farmer in Welgeval. Khwiti also agreed that there was no point in leaving her little shop to start all over again. So the conditions for Davidson's retirement were set.

Two years later, Mangope accepted "independence" for his homeland on a persuasive ticket for those not inclined to radical politics. He was a fiery and clever speaker, who easily left even his opponents with food for thought. He argued that, if a small country like Lesotho and the smallest European nation state such as Luxembourg could be independent, why couldn't Bophuthatswana have a mind of its own and take advantage of the present policies to develop the Batswana? He proceeded to put together a cabinet, and offered his old inspector Davidson a position as deputy minister.

The radical left, however, argued that any individual who cooperated with the apartheid government by accepting the homeland policies was essentially a traitor. This presented a problem for Davidson.

"With our radical children, how can I accept this post?" he confided to his wife.

"Since when, my dear, do we have to get our children's permission to make decisions?" Khwiti replied.

Davidson mulled over the dilemma for days.

"Do they expect us to sit and twiddle our toes on the stoep when we can take the opportunity to influence things from inside?" he said with a changed tune.

"That would be very silly of us," the wife agreed.

And so Davidson accepted the post.

"How could you do this to me?" his son thundered from across the borders, deeply embarrassed by his father's decision.

"What did I do to you?" Davidson replied. "Did you ever consult me when you planned your involvements?"

A family feud was declared, and each camp caught the flak of the other's involvements. The children's radical credentials were blemished, while the father was viewed as too unreliable for a full ministerial position. But, in spite of this schizophrenic life, somehow the clan swam along, kept together by the original bonds that had grown out of Welgeval.

45

By the time Davidson took office in Bophuthatswana, the consultants were ready with their findings for economic development. By a nasty twist of fate, Davidson was appointed deputy minister for economic development, and the consultants identified the scenic Pilanesberg as the most profitable area for development.

Like those who had come before them, they stood in awe of the twisted mountains and fertile valleys of the region; they marvelled at the rocky outcrops and patches of granite spills; and admired the thickets of karee, wild olive, *Mongela* and *Mmilo* trees that covered the area, setting it apart from the rest of Bophuthatswana.

Apart from its beauty, the Pilanesberg area was centrally located and in close proximity to the potential tourism market of the Johannesburg metropolis. Situated in the centre of a one-hundred-million-year-old volcano, one of the largest of its kind, the Pilanesberg mountains also had unique geological features, which could provide a range of habitats for different types of animals.

But the area also had potential of a less natural variety. Gambling was banned in South Africa, and any citizens with disposable income and a love of the casino frittered their money away in the nearby state of Swaziland. And so a local gambling niche was also identified in the homeland. The team recommended the establishment of a holiday and gambling resort for tourists and a game conservation park in the area.

The Bophuthatswana government teamed up with property developer Sol Kerzner, who established the resort of Sun City, while the government developed the Pilanesberg game reserve alongside.

The government bought out all the farmers in the valley and negotiated the incorporation of Welgeval into the game park. A royalty agreement was drawn up with Chief Pilane of the Bakgatla, who now possessed the title deed for Welgeval. The chief agreed to the deal, as the project seemed to hold significant economic benefits for the Bakgatla. In the flurry of development, the age-old agreement for the Welgevalers' continued stay on the farm was swiftly forgotten.

Davidson was slapped right in the middle of a dilemma – his new job on the one side, and Welgeval, his home, on the other. We can only imagine his reaction at the presentation of the findings.

"Let's not do it there," he declared. "My people live in that area."

"Gentlemen, we must not get personal about these things. Think about the development of our people, the people of Bophuthatswana."

"But my people have lived there for generations."

"Mr Moloto, your people will be compensated for the houses they have built. Besides, they will be moved to an area near the budding town of Mogwase. We already have incentives and a tax-break programme that will bring factories and all sorts of industry to the area. Your people will get jobs and they'll be able to educate their children."

"But it's not just about the houses we've built ..."

"Mr Moloto, you know that farm is not really yours ..."

In the month of June 1980 the Bophuthatswana government sent out emissaries to deliver notices of removal to the farm's inhabitants, and all the Welgevalers were summoned from the various corners of South Africa to come and pack up their belongings and collect their animals. Later in the month, a government messenger arrived once again, this time to deliver envelopes containing minimum compensation for the houses that now stood ready to be destroyed. In rebellion against relocation to an area of the government's choice, some people moved to villages of their own selection.

Finally, one Thursday morning in August 1980, government lorries rolled in to finish off the removal. Those who had stayed until the end watched as the vehicles lumbered up to the highest point of Welgeval and pushed their way through the Malau family residence, which was situated above the other houses.

The people of Welgeval gathered round to witness the destruction brought on to them. Women cried and clung to each other as the walls tumbled down. To avoid their own emotions, the men impatiently called them to pull themselves together and help load furniture onto the lorries. Officials in blue overalls handed out tents after each house was demolished.

The bulldozers worked their way down the slopes to the flat land, leaving piles of rubble in their wake. The church and the school at the centre of the farm were the next to fall, leaving only the modest monument built for the centenary of Gonin's arrival. This sent out stronger shock waves than the demolition of the homes. These buildings had housed all of Welgeval's memories – every important event took place here. The big wild olive tree stood lone once more, stripped of its holy status, just as it had been in the beginning before all these people had arrived.

The Welgevalers watched to see if the mighty bulldozers would head for the graveyard across the river where Polomane, Christina, Ryk Kerneels and all the first inhabitants were buried. But their appetite for dust was satisfied and they crawled back whence they came.

Early that evening, lorries packed with furniture, small animals and women trundled out of Welgeval, the hills throwing back at them the din of screaming pigs and barking dogs.

"Kom, Swartland!"

A man cracked a whip to urge the cattle out of Welgeval for the very last time.

EPILOGUE

By the time they arrived in Sandfontein, a flat barren piece of land of no comparison to Welgeval, some of the pigs had died of exhaustion. The men piled them to the side and started pitching tents for the families, anxious to make the most of the fading light. They managed to pack some furniture into the tents, but left much of it standing outside, hoping to make decent settlement plans the next day. Then they crawled into their tents to sleep. In the thick of the dust stirred up by the arriving and departing lorries, and perhaps too stunned by their dislocation, the Welgevalers had not noticed the storm gathering in the sky. It burst open just after they had settled down on the hard ground, welcoming them to Sandfontein. Fearing a flood and the collapse of their wobbly tents, they got up from the ground and sat on the boxes, dozing now and again until sunrise when the rain stopped. The furniture that was standing outside the tents was soaked and destroyed.

The exiles from Welgeval had plots of land allotted to them and a few months later they had built brick houses – low-cost flat tin-roofed makeshifts to call home. They even dared to name the new place Welgeval, but it bore no resemblance: the flat open landscape and sandy soil were a daily reminder of their loss, evoking feelings of humiliation and shame as time went on. The houses were too close to one another; you could be seen from the street. The real Welgeval was an idyll of seclusion and choice: you saw your neighbour only when you wanted. This exposure! The older settlers could not adjust to the wrench from their land and their old lifestyle. Many of them soon died – one after another.

Thank God some of the people of Welgeval survived. As soon as the resettlement programme was announced and confirmed, the big cattle farmers decided to go to villages where there was abundant grazing veld. Their lifestyles did not change too much. Others opted to settle in towns and cities, and some retained their itinerant farming wherever they could find land. In the new Welgeval, life had shrunk to a dreariness whose main occupation was waiting for government grants, pensions and remittances from those working in the cities. The few goats and pigs that survived the trek wandered around all day, picking up bits of grass and plastic here and there – disorientated from all the strangeness.

The year 1994 brought in a new government to South Africa and a new dispensation in which all are equal before the law. Redress of past injustices became an important policy of the ANC government. The Land Commission and the Land Claims Court were established to provide victims of forced removals an opportunity to apply for restitution of the land they had lost. The Department of Agriculture and Land Affairs led the land restitution process. They made a call for claims and assisted communities in filling the claim forms. My cousins led by John Moloto formed a claims committee with representatives of the nine families that had bought Welgeval and filed a claim. This proved to be the easiest part of the land restitution process, however. The claimants had to provide evidence of ownership of the land they were claiming. They were stuck, not knowing where to find such evidence, because they did not have the title deed. Looking for evidence was especially difficult for a community that had lost so much stuff in the process of resettlement. Many communities that submitted claims gave up at this point because they could not produce evidence for their claim. By a fortunate coincidence, I

Epilogue

had just finished my research for this book when I learnt about my cousins' predicament. I had found papers documenting the history of ownership of Welgeval, from Gonin to the later inhabitants. My cousin Moloko and I then joined the claims committee to lend a hand. I quickly put together the required evidence and we submitted.

Our claims were gazetted on 19 November 2004 and we were immediately asked to form a Communal Property Association (CPA), which would be a decision-making body on matters related to the claim and, in future, on all matters relating to the Pilanesberg National Park, in which the original Welgeval was situated. We called all the remaining relatives of the original nine buyers to form a CPA. The Department then took us through the process of electing an executive committee which would represent the larger CPA in negotiations with the North West Parks and Tourism Board and officials from the Department of Agriculture and Land Affairs. To ensure equal representation of all families, we structured the executive so that it included one representative from each of the nine families. This structure proved to be successful, because we have not had any fights between families to date.

We later learnt that two claims for Welgeval had been submitted. The chief of the Bakgatla had submitted claims for several farms inside the Pilanesberg National Park, including Welgeval. The Department had to reconcile this duplication of the Welgeval claim. They organised a series of meetings between the Welgeval and Bakgatla CPAs to discuss the legitimacy of our claims. The Welgeval CPA came to these discussions as underdogs – mere subjects confronting the tribe, which was armed with a lawyer to argue its case. The Bakgatla argued that they were in possession of the Welgeval title deed and were therefore the legitimate claimants. But we were not intimidated. Having acquired all the harrowing information about the origins of our ancestors, we were highly motivated to finally get justice for them.

We argued that lodging a claim for Welgeval was the bare minimum we could do in order to address the injustices meted out to our ancestors. Should we perhaps have started with the Truth and Reconciliation Commission before coming here? If the purpose of the land restitution programme was to redress injustices relating to land ownership, our claim should take priority because, unlike the Bakgatla, who were just claiming a piece of land, our claim involved the loss of a home, livelihood and land.

We also argued that our ancestors could have approached other people to lend them money to pay off the farm, but they had agreed to Chief Ramono Pilane's help because he was one of the original nine buyers and the son-in-law of Stephanus Maja Moloto. They considered him one of them. They trusted that with his help their future on Welgeval was secure.

The law at the time was also not on their side. While they were buying Welgeval after Gonin's departure, there was a looming threat of eviction, as they were considered to be "tenant farmers" – black people farming on white people's land – a practice that was discouraged by the 1913 Land Act. Decades later, the Bophuthatswana government put the final nail in the coffin and physically removed us from our home. This was a definite result of an unjust, politically motivated decision. How many times should our people be dispossessed?

We had some heated discussions, but they were tempered by the fact that there were criss-crossing relations between the people of Welgeval and Bakgatla, and so underneath the hot words, there was sympathy to our point of view. The Department took time to hear and evaluate all arguments and then departed to submit the two points of view for adjudication by the Land Commission.

While we were waiting for the verdict, my cousin Sam – Polomane's great-grandson and our virtual chief – made acquaintance

Epilogue

with a woman from the village of Moletji in Limpopo province, where our ancestors originally came from. She told him that every year on the 16 December public holiday, the Moloto clan there has an annual reunion feast. Sam decided to join her on her next trip to the clan meeting so that he could introduce the Molotos from Rustenburg to the main clan. Sam was warmly received, and he was given an opportunity to introduce himself and the Rustenburg Moloto clan. He also promised to bring more members of his clan for a special visit.

As soon as Sam came back, we began to plan a trip for September 2006. We agreed to bring presents – a blanket for the queen mother and copies of this book for both the chief and the premier of Limpopo, Sello Moloto. On 15 September, at about five in the morning, eleven of us set off on our first pilgrimage to Moletji. We didn't sleep much the previous night: wrapping presents, preparing provisions and enjoying the excitement of our first trip to the almost mythical Moletji. We kept asking ourselves how our ancestors could have felt trapped in Rustenburg, which was only 400 kilometres from Moletji – why did they not escape and go back home? On second thought we realised that this question was only reasonable to a free adult. I recalled the control and limitations on *inboekelings'* lives as described in Eldredge and Morton's book. Our ancestors were not free to make such choices. Morton quotes an observer who states: "*I never saw a full-grown Kafir sold, and they are reputed to be free, but in case of endeavoring to escape are caught and punished.*"[1] The cost of trying to escape must have been very high, and because they were captured as young children, they must have adjusted to life on the farms. Their journey from their Moletji to Rustenburg on ox-wagons and on foot must have seemed so long that by the time they arrived, they were completely disorientated and could not trace their way back home. An observation made by British official Morrison Barlow in

1881 puts into perspective the estrangement of people like our ancestors from their homes:

> *I have come across that peculiar class of servant who receive no pay of any kind or description; they get their food given to them and their clothes. When I asked them where they came from, they say they have been with their master ever since they were quite small. I have said to them, "where are your father and mother?" "I do not know; I have never seen them." "where do you come from?" "I do not know." I have seen scores and scores of cases like that …*[2]

We finally appreciated the predicament of our ancestors and felt honoured for the privilege to complete the cycle and find the way back home on their behalf.

We arrived at the chief's court in Moletji at about nine in the morning, and the place was abuzz with people preparing for the feast to welcome us. We knew that they were expecting us, but we did not for a minute think that the proverbial fatted cow would be slaughtered for us. To say we were touched would be an understatement, but we did not have much time to react to what we saw. An old woman and an old man met us at the entrance and they took the women and men in our party to separate rondavels in the yard. At the women's rondavel, we found four old women sitting on mats scattered on the floor, waiting for us. There was not a stick of furniture in the room. The old women asked us to join them on the floor and we obeyed and sat down. We tried to greet them and introduce ourselves, but we were told to sit quietly for a while. We sat there silent, with only the thudding of our hearts and the throbbing of the strange but familiar ground beneath us. Tears welled up in our eyes, but seeing the impassive faces of our hosts calmed us down. The reason for this silent interlude was never explained to us and we

Epilogue

were too modest to ask, but we surmised that it was meant to allow us to clock in with our local ancestors.

After about fifteen minutes, one of the old women greeted us and we then introduced ourselves and started chatting. The waiters outside took their cue from the sound of our voices and brought us tea and delicious scones. When we finished, we were asked to go out of the yard again so that we could be formally received. A traditional band of horn players started playing and women sang, ululating as we were led in again. This time we went to sit in the amphitheatre where the chief officiates at tribal functions such as the one we had that day. Then Premier Sello Moloto welcomed us, not as premier of the province but as a member of the Moloto clan, which he said had gathered to welcome us to Moletji. He said he had heard of the Molotos of Rustenburg but had never met any of them. Sam, our senior, was then given a chance to introduce each one of us and to express our gratitude for the very warm welcome we had received. Finally, Chief Moloto gave a short speech to welcome us. We strained our ears to hear if anyone remembered the day the children left Moletji, but nothing was said in that regard. But to be plunged into the larger pool of Molotos was most edifying indeed. We felt endorsed and strengthened to the depths of our souls.

A few months after our visit, the Department of Agriculture and Land Affairs called the Bakgatla and Welgeval CPAs to a meeting to deliver the Land Commission's verdict on our two claims. The official from the Department announced that the Land Commission had decided that the Bakgatla had not been dispossessed of land in this case, as they had only helped to buy Welgeval. They also did not meet certain requirements of the Restitution Act, and their claim was dismissed by the Commission. Legal advisors of both CPAs were then asked to meet and negotiate compensation for the Bakgatlas' contribution to the purchase of Welgeval. After a lot of toing and froing, it was decided that the Bakgatla would constitute the tenth family in the Welgeval CPA. That meant that whatever benefit we got from the Parks Board, we would divide by ten and no longer by nine. Registration of the settlement was lodged with the state attorney on 23 November 2007. All successful CPAs then started a process of developing Settlement Agreements with the national and provincial Departments of Agriculture and Land Affairs and the North West Parks and Tourism Board. The agreement emphasised the fact that the Welgeval community cannot be resettled in their original land or use it as before, because it now lies inside a conservation area which is a national asset. It identified the privileges and rights that the community could enjoy inside the park, such as site visits with proper arrangements with the park officials and the right to participate in approved viable economic development projects based on the park's strategic plans. The detail of these privileges and rights were to be further outlined in a second agreement called the Co-Management Agreement, which would be signed with the Parks Board.

On 23 February 2008 the Minister of Agriculture and Land Affairs called a big meeting to hand over title deeds to all CPAs whose claims of land in the Pilanesberg National Park were successful. In preparation for the meeting, the Welgeval community, who were ever so happy to receive the title deed, donated a cow towards food to be served after the meeting and collected money for refreshments. They also erected a memorial stone, with the names of the Claims Committee engraved on it, which now stands inside the park at the old site of Welgeval, under the old wild olive tree that was the first Dutch Reformed Church and next to the memorial stone of the centenary of the Dutch Reformed Church in the Transvaal (which can be found on the map of Pilanesberg National Park). The minister announced a few financial packages for compensation and

Epilogue

development, and the first we got was R25 000 per family as compensation for what was called "loss of joy". While we appreciated the gesture, the amount was so small that it caused more "loss of joy" in families where the beneficiaries comprised the fourth or fifth generation from the original buyers. "It is better than nothing," our people consoled themselves, as the money trickled down the generations. We maintain that benefits from our land claim will only make sense when the Parks Board sincerely facilitates the implementation of the Co-Management Agreement we have now signed, and we develop projects that consider our present needs.

Although the slow bureaucratic processes in implementing our agreements with the provincial Parks and Tourism Board are often frustrating, we are grateful for the confident swagger we acquired, ever since our land claim was approved. We may not have physically resettled on Welgeval, but we are now officially recognised as co-owners of the Pilanesberg National Park. Our Settlement Agreement states that this ownership can never be sold, and this ensures that future generations of the people of Welgeval will benefit from this land restitution. In addition, we have reconnected with the main Moloto clan in Moletji. We hope that all these developments will compensate, even in a tiny measure, for the hardships our ancestors suffered. May this story forever be a source of strength for us and our children in times of life's challenges.

ACKNOWLEDGEMENTS

Among the many people who contributed to the completion of this book, I would like to thank Felicity Levine for introducing me to writing that is not mere "fact dumping" and for editing my drafts, free of charge. Thank you to my cousin Moloko Nke for believing in the project of documenting our people's story and joining me on the search for information from all the Moloto "oldies". I'm grateful to my friend Susan Newton-King for setting me in the right direction to answer all the questions about Welgeval. I'm thankful for the serendipitous meeting with Fred Morton which supported my quest. Deep gratitude is reserved for former Minister of Agriculture and Land Affairs Lulu Xingwana and her team for restoring Welgeval to us.

NOTES

PROLOGUE

1 Fred Morton, "Captive Labor in the Western Transvaal After the Sand River Convention", in Elizabeth A. Eldredge and Fred Morton (eds.), *Slavery in South Africa: Captive Labor on the Dutch Frontier* (Boulder, Colorado: Westview Press, 1994), p. 179.

2 Jan C.A. Boeyens, "'Black Ivory': The Indenture System and Slavery in Zoutpansberg, 1848–1869", in Eldredge and Morton (eds.) *Slavery in South Africa*, p. 201

3 Morton, "Captive Labor in the Western Transvaal After the Sand River Convention", p. 167.

4 Boeyens, "Black Ivory", p. 204.

EPILOGUE

1 Morton, "Captive Labor in the Western Transvaal After the Sand River Convention".

2 Quoted in Boeyens, "Black Ivory", pp. 205–6.